AN EVALUATION OF CHILD WITNESS SUPPORT

Joyce Plotnikoff and Richard Woolfson
Consultants

Scottish Executive Central Research Unit
2001

Further copies of this report are available priced £5.00. Cheques should be made payable to The Stationery Office Ltd and addressed to:

> The Stationery Office Bookshop
> 71 Lothian Road
> Edinburgh
> EH3 9AZ
>
> Tel: 0131-228-4181
> Fax: 0131-622 7017

The views expressed in this report are those of the researchers and do not necessarily represent those of the Department or Scottish Ministers.

© Crown Copyright 2001
Limited extracts from the text may be produced provided the source is acknowledged. For more extensive reproduction, please write to the Chief Research Officer at the Central Research Unit, Saughton House, Broomhouse Drive, Edinburgh EH11 3XA

CONTENTS

INTRODUCTION 7
    PHASE ONE 7
    PHASE TWO 10
    THE LAYOUT OF THE REPORT 10

METHODOLOGY 11

PROFILE OF THE PILOT CASES 16
    THE CHILDREN 16
    THE ACCUSED 16
    THE CASES 16
    HOW LONG THEY TOOK 17
    MEDICAL EXAMINATIONS 18

SUPPORT AND PREPARATION OF YOUNG WITNESSES 21
    PHASE ONE FINDINGS 21
    PHASE TWO 34

COMMUNICATION OF INFORMATION ABOUT YOUNG WITNESSES WITHIN THE JUSTICE SYSTEM 42
    PHASE ONE FINDINGS 42
    PHASE TWO 51

IDENTIFICATION OF THE ACCUSED 60
    PHASE ONE FINDINGS 60
    PHASE TWO 62

INTERVIEWS AND PRECOGNITIONS 73
    PHASE ONE FINDINGS 73
    PHASE TWO 77

EVALUATION OF THE CHILD WITNESS INITIATIVE 88
    SUPPORT AND PREPARATION PILOT 82
    THE COMMUNICATIONS PILOT 94
    THE IDENTIFICATION PILOT 96
    THE PRECOGNITION AND INTERVIEWS PILOT 98
    THE RESOURCE IMPLICATIONS OF THE PILOT PROJECTS 99
    EVALUATION OF THE PROCESS BY WHICH THE WORKING GROUP DEVELOPED AND IMPLEMENTED THE PILOT INITIATIVES 101

CONCLUSION 104
    UNDERLYING PRESUMPTIONS ABOUT THE TREATMENT OF CHILD WITNESSES IN SCOTLAND 104
    THE WAY FORWARD 105

ANNEX A: Address to the jury in cases in the sheriff court involving a child witness 107
ANNEX B: The Lord Advocate's Working Group: Report and Recommendations 110

LIST OF TABLES

Table 1: Model of an integrated child witness support structure 8

Table 2: Numbers of interviews and responses to questionnaires 13

Table 3: Problems identified during Phase One concerning communication of information about young witnesses 49

Table 4: Relationship to the accused and identification parades 64

Table 5: Number of times children were spoken to about the alleged offence 81

INTRODUCTION

PHASE ONE

In September 1995, we were commissioned by the Scottish Office Central Research Unit to assist the Lord Advocate's Working Group on child witness support. Our work was based in Glasgow and was carried out in two phases, from October 1995 to March 1996, and between April 1996 and August 1998. The research objectives in Phase One were:

- to map current professional practice, structures and relationships, and identify examples of good practice
- to identify the needs of child witnesses
- to identify mechanisms for the improvement of practice and procedures and a transitional path for putting such improvements into practice
- to produce a plan for a pilot initiative.

The Phase One mapping exercise identified a wide range of child witness policies in which certain good practice principles were common to all organisations. Nevertheless, the overall picture suggested that only certain categories of young witnesses were likely to receive support, and that responsibilities for support, liaison, information flow and monitoring were poorly defined. There was a need to bring elements of good practice together into an integrated child witness support structure that would augment the services available to young witnesses without undermining the existing responsibilities of individual organisations. The research report presented to the Working Group at the end of Phase One suggested that the building blocks of such a structure should include:

- documentation which made clear the child witness policies and procedures of individual organisations
- agreements between organisations to coordinate procedures in relation to young witnesses
- codes of good practice for the legal profession
- guidance describing the scope of appropriate support and preparation of the child for court
- explanatory materials for young witnesses and their parents or carers[1]
- information for the judiciary about young witnesses

We concluded that the key to the creation of an integrated child witness support structure was an independent child witness support officer (CWO) to act as a central information point for information and advice for those working directly with young witnesses, and who would also prepare for court some children who would not otherwise receive this service. NCH Action for Children and Children 1st agreed to fund the experimental CWO position on a part-time basis for one year during Phase Two of the project.

---

[1] The Crown Office booklets 'Going to Court as a Witness?' for the age-groups five to 12 and 12 to 16 were published in 1998

The components of the integrated child witness support model are summarised in the following table:

Table 1: Model of an integrated child witness support structure, based on findings in Phase One of the research

Module	Objective	Underpinning findings from Phase 1
Individual organisations' child witness policies and procedures	To document each organisation's policies and procedures in relation to training, resource allocation and monitoring of service	Within departments, practice was often inconsistent. There was confusion about certain policies, for example those relating to children's identification evidence, and whether therapy was permissible prior to the child giving evidence at court
Service level agreements between organisations	To clarify what agencies can expect from one another and provide a basis for inter-agency monitoring	Despite strong policy commitments to inter-agency consultation, 'rubbing points' arose as a result of confusion about respective roles and boundaries. For example, there was a common policy to expedite child witness cases but no system for flagging or monitoring them as they moved through the system. No statistics were collected. Best practice on the co-ordination of forensic medical examinations called for them to be carried out in hospital facilities but in 1995, 75% of sexual abuse examinations were conducted on police premises
Guidance on good practice for the legal profession	To clarify what constitutes good practice in contact with and examination of child witnesses and to contribute to legal education	Examples of poor practice related to the conduct of precognition, particularly by unqualified and unmonitored agents, the use of inappropriate language during cross-examination, and an inconsistent approach to child witnesses by advocates depute
Guidance for practitioners on the support and preparation of child witnesses	To specify what constitutes appropriate support and preparation	Pre-trial preparation was limited in both time and content. Practitioners recognised the importance of not contaminating the child's evidence but the absence of guidance and the lack of clear boundaries curtailed what they felt they could do

Guidance for child witnesses and parents/ carers	To provide more explanatory materials about the legal process	The Crown Office leaflet 'Going to Court' was being revised but there were no materials for parents and carers of child witnesses in criminal proceedings or for children attending children's hearing court hearings
Information for the judiciary	To inform discretionary decision-making and ensure that children's needs are addressed	Judges and sheriffs were often notified about child witness cases at the last minute. This hindered planning and delayed consideration of the need to modify procedures. They received no feedback about measures that worked well or aspects of the process which children found stressful. They had no training, guidance or formal opportunity to exchange views about each others' practice. The Lord Justice General's Memorandum (1990) advises judges to take account of children's individual circumstances before deciding whether to modify procedures to minimise anxiety or distress. In the absence of formal mechanisms for the transfer of child-related information to the judge or sheriff at trial, members of the judiciary were circumspect about receiving such information.
Child witness officer	To augment existing arrangements by appointing an independent person to work with child witnesses, develop good practice and facilitate communication between agencies and with parents/ carers	There was little evidence of 'new and improved' support provisions as urged by the Scottish Law Commission. Pre-trial preparation was available only to restricted categories of children. Police officers, procurators fiscal, social workers and those in the voluntary sector described inter-agency co-ordination as poor. They felt unable to provide an adequate level of support and preparation

PHASE TWO

Phase Two of the study began in April 1996. The Working Group agreed to conduct five pilot exercises that took forward specific aspects of the proposed child witness support structure. These pilots concerned:

- support and preparation of young witnesses for court
- the position of child witness officer
- the evidence of young witnesses concerning identification of the accused
- communication in the legal process of information about the child witness
- interviews and precognitions, and the number of times the child is asked to discuss the circumstances of the alleged offence.

The aims of the research in Phase Two were to:

- support the sub-groups for each of the pilots
- establish the extent to which the pilot initiatives met their objectives
- assess the resource implications of implementing the initiatives on a wider scale
- describe the role played by the organisations involved and the extent to which the best practice applied in the pilots varied from normal practice
- ascertain the views of practitioners and (where appropriate) children and their parents or carers about their experience
- evaluate the process by which the Working Group developed and implemented the pilot initiatives.

THE LAYOUT OF THE REPORT

The next two chapters describe the study methodology and give details about the cases monitored in Phase Two. Each of the five chapters which follow describe key concerns identified during Phase One and the implementation of the corresponding pilot in Phase Two.

The penultimate chapter draws together the findings from the pilots to highlight the key evaluation findings. It assesses the extent to which the pilots met their objectives, describes the resource implications of pilot implementation and evaluates the effectiveness of the Working Group. The final chapter considers some of the underlying presumptions about the treatment of child witnesses in Scotland. This discussion sets the context for the recommendations of the Lord Advocate's Working Group.

METHODOLOGY

The Phase One mapping exercise took place between October 1995 and March 1996. It consisted of a review of policy and practice documents, questionnaire surveys, interviews, and a detailed inter-agency study of four closed cases. This work formed the basis of proposals for the pilot initiatives. Phase Two, carried out between April 1996 and August 1998, covered the planning of the pilots and their implementation. Questionnaires, interviews and observation were used to assess their effectiveness. A total of 320 interviews were conducted during both phases of the study.

It had been hoped that the pilots would be underway by the start of 1997 but progress was slower than planned because of major local government reorganisation and changes in membership of the Working Group. As a result, subgroup action plans and protocols were not completed until May 1998.

During Phase Two, the research team supported the development of the pilot initiatives by preparing discussion papers drawing on recent developments in published and unpublished child witness research and practice in England and Wales and elsewhere.

The Working Group agreed that the research team would assess not only the development of the pilot procedures but also their implementation. A small number of cases were identified for this purpose, to avoid imposing too heavy a burden on participants who were being asked to adopt new procedures and to allow the cases to be studied in detail. By the end of Phase Two, 26 cases involving a total of 66 children had been monitored, and 190 interviews had been conducted. These case studies enabled the research team to evaluate the process of implementing change across the pilots. In addition, 32 young witnesses in non-pilot cases were observed giving evidence at court.

The Group's discussions about the volume and throughput of child witness cases were hindered by the lack of statistics or system for flagging up such cases. The number of witnesses under 16 was not monitored by the police, procurator fiscal or reporter. Referrals to the identification pilot began in May 1997 but other pilots did not receive referrals until September 1997. The Group had estimated that cases need be drawn from only two police divisions, and initially only their personnel were briefed. When insufficient cases were identified a further four police divisions were briefed about the project and case referrals continued until May 1998. Reporter referrals were included in the pilot terms of reference but none were received.

Eleven of the 26 monitored cases were referred to the pilot with the joint aims of improving inter-agency communication about the child witness and reducing the total number of times children were asked to give an account of the alleged offence during interviews and precognitions. The same cases were monitored for both aspects of the joint pilot on the basis that improved communication at an early stage might assist in meeting the information and assessment needs of the professionals involved. Eight cases were assigned to the pilot on support and preparation at the point when it seemed likely that a child would need to give evidence. Seven cases were assigned to the identification pilot.

During Phase Two, the research team observed a wide range of court proceedings involving pilot and non-pilot cases, as well as identification parades, children's pre-trial visits to the court, case discussions and conferences chaired by the social work department. Examples of practice observed at court are listed at the end of this section.

The research brief for Phase One did not call for direct contact with children and families, though a small number of families were seen in interviews with voluntary organisations. In Phase Two, the Working Group agreed that in identification pilot cases, carers and children could be interviewed after participation in the parade. On behalf of the researchers, the police also contacted some parents and carers of children in other pilot cases and asked them to keep a record of the number of times the child was interviewed. However, it was generally felt more appropriate to defer interviews until after cases were completed. A total of 23 carers and 11 children were interviewed. Because 12 cases were still pending when the fieldwork finished, this aspect of our study was curtailed. We were therefore grateful to Kathleen Murray for an analysis of 71 pre-trial interviews with carers and post-trial interviews with 37 carers and 56 children that had been conducted as part of her research on CCTV. Her report was commissioned by the Scottish Office on behalf of the Working Group and is referred to in the body of our report.[2] The families reported by Murray and those to whom we spoke made observations on the legal process which were very similar.

---

[2] Preparing Child Witnesses for Court (1997) Scottish Office

Table 2: Numbers of interviews and responses to questionnaires

Category of interviewee	Phase 1	Phase 2
prosecution (fiscals, precognition officers, Crown Office staff, advocates depute)	11	22
social work personnel (managers, social workers, family support unit staff, trainer, department solicitor)	30	28
police officers	16	35
reporters	11	18
judges	4	-
sheriffs	4	8
safeguarders/ curators ad litem	6	4
other solicitors	10	10
paediatricians, psychiatrists, psychologists, other hospital staff	10	4
court personnel (district court, sheriff court, High Court)	8	8
teachers	4	8
police surgeons	3	4
voluntary sector groups	13	7
carers	-	23
children	-	11
TOTAL	130	190

Examples of practice observed at court during the course of the study

Examples of good practice:

- The sheriff criticising arrangements which meant the children had long waits at court

- Allowing the child and carer to wait in a secure area and giving the carer a magnetic 'swipe' card so she could fetch refreshments from the cafeteria

- Asking the child whether he/she wants the sheriff and lawyers to remove their wigs and gowns

- Enabling a witness to act as supporter to the child by allowing him/her to give evidence first

- The sheriff advising the child to speak slowly and not to shrug or nod because 'I have to write down what you say'

- The sheriff agreeing to allow a nervous child who is having trouble speaking to answer only 'yes' or 'no' questions

- intervention by the procurator fiscal when the child is having difficulty with the question

- the sheriff allowing the child to have a break when he has difficulty concentrating

- the sheriff directing the questioner to move on after repetitive questions

- the sheriff telling the defence solicitor that it is inappropriate to ask the child about dates 15 months in the past

- The sheriff asking the questioner to check whether a child has understood a question

- The sheriff saying 'thank you' to the child when testimony is over

Problems arising in observed cases:

- Procurators fiscal failing to turn up at scheduled appointments for pre-trial court visits

- The person taking the pre-court visit being unaware of the crèche facility and telling families that there is no CCTV at the sheriff court

- The person taking the pre-court visit saying to the children that they should not be afraid because the accused 'looks like an alright man'. The children were still angry about this comment weeks afterwards

- The parent having to remind the procurator fiscal that the children's address is given as care of the police station

- Children waiting in public areas
- Children precognosced by the defence during an adjournment on the day of trial
- Children being asked to give their address aloud at the start of their testimony
- Children and carers unaware that the procurator fiscal cannot speak to them once they have started to give evidence
- Children thinking they are at fault because they were given no explanation about why they had to leave the courtroom during legal argument
- One child about to give evidence on CCTV seeing her sister come out of the CCTV room in floods of tears; the carer said this was so harrowing that the second child was too upset to answer coherently
- The defence lawyer moving to stand by the accused while the child gives evidence, in the courtroom, making the child look towards the accused while answering questions[3]
- the defence lawyer asking an autistic child to do multiplication tables and how many days there are in five months
- The child seeing the procurator fiscal and defence lawyer 'laughing and joking' together after the case was over: 'They could at least wait until we'd left'
- A child who gave evidence to support an application for a child protection order at 8p.m. said 'The sheriff spoke to me as if I was a nuisance and said "I can't understand why you're suddenly afraid of this man". It made me cry'
- The movement-sensitive lights going out in the CCTV room while an eight year-old gave evidence. Afterwards she said 'I knew it was Uncle A's [the accused's] magic that put the lights out'.

---

[3] 'Attorneys should question children from a single, neutral location. Walking round the room creates a changing visual backdrop that distratcs children. Standing near the defendant creates emotional factors that could hamper the child's ability to testify to the best of his or her ability': J. Myers et al (1996) Psychological Research on Children as Witnesses: Practical Implications for Forensic Interviews and Courtroom Testimony. Pacific Law Journal Vol. 27, pp. 1-82

PROFILE OF THE PILOT CASES

THE CHILDREN

The 26 pilot cases involved a total of 66 children ranging in age from four to 16: 31 boys with an average age of nine, and 35 girls with an average age of 10. Twenty-one of the 26 cases concerned sexual offences; 16 involved complaints of offences over a period of time (seven of a year or longer). Forty-seven of the children were victims and 19 were bystander witnesses, mostly in relation to a sexual offence on another child. The reporting officer in 17 of the 21 sexual offence cases was a member of a police Female and Child Unit (FACU). A social worker was present at FACU interviews in six cases.

Sexual offences were one of the criteria for case selection, so their preponderance in the pilot should not be seen as significant. In a previous study of child witnesses cited in criminal proceedings in Glasgow, the majority were bystander witnesses to assaults or breaches of the peace. Only about 10 per cent of charges in that study related to sexual offences.[4]

Children in 21 pilot cases were referred to the reporter. In 14 cases there had been a previous referral and children in five were already in care; others were the subjects of voluntary or compulsory supervision. Case discussions were held in eight cases and child protection procedures were initiated in three cases. Children in three pilot cases were removed from home.

THE ACCUSED

All but one of the 26 persons accused was male. In ten cases, he was a member of the household; in another ten, he was a relative or otherwise well known to the child. Five cases involved strangers. The age of the accused ranged between 16 and 72 with an average of 37. Fourteen were initially remanded in custody, of which four were in custody throughout the pre-trial period. Conditions not to contact the witnesses were imposed on all those bailed.

THE CASES

Sixteen pilot cases began on petition, procedure for prosecuting more serious cases. Six of these were assigned to the High Court, five were sheriff and jury matters and five were eventually disposed of by summary procedure. A further five cases were dealt with by summary procedure from the outset. Of the remaining five, the procurator fiscal decided not to proceed in three and in the others, investigations were still ongoing at the end of fieldwork.

---

[4] R. Flin et al. (1993) Child witnesses in Scottish criminal trials. International Review of Victimology, 2, 309-329

Eleven cases reached a final hearing at court. Six resulted in a guilty plea and four in a guilty verdict. A custodial sentence was imposed in five of these ten convictions. One summary trial resulted in an acquittal when the complainer failed to speak to his previous statement.

Excluding cases that had been withdrawn or had not reached precognition, applications for CCTV had been made on behalf of 12 child witnesses (24 per cent). This proportion was probably higher than normal because of the selection of sexual offence cases. In the CCTV experiment that began in 1991, the Crown lodged applications on behalf of 10 per cent of child witnesses over a 27-month period.[5] Since then, High Court applications recorded nationally have been reported at around 20 per year from 1995 through the first half of 1998. Recent figures from Glasgow Sheriff Court indicated a similar level of applications.[6]

HOW LONG THEY TOOK

An analysis was made of how long pilot cases took at each stage. Crown Office policy required child witness cases to be given priority. Procurators fiscal had specific case management responsibilities to:

- expedite cases at marking and precognition
- give advance notice to the Crown Office High Court unit of cases in which High Court proceedings are contemplated
- liase with the court to ensure an early trial diet and that the case is timetabled to proceed without deferring to custody cases fixed for the same day
- make 'strenuous efforts' to avoid adjournments of the trial diet.[7]

Despite the policy to expedite, no statistics were routinely collected about the pace of child witness cases.[8] There was no precise definition of cases to which the 'fast track' policy applied. High Court child witness cases were often taken out of the trial list but the Crown Office High Court unit did not maintain a separate log to monitor how often this happened.

Seventeen pilot cases were reported to the police on the day of the offence or within ten days. The remaining nine cases were reported to the police from four weeks to almost four years after the offence, on average over a year later.

The police are expected to submit a report to the procurator fiscal within three weeks of the offence being reported to the police. Officers reported 12 cases to the procurator fiscal within a week. Eight cases were reported from three to nine weeks later and six cases were reported

---

[5] K. Murray (1995) Live Television Link

[6] Figures were provided by the Scottish Court Service. Data collection forms have been redesigned due to inconsistencies in recording in previous years. SCS advised that previous figures reflecting actual usage had been unreliable

[7] Book of Regulations 16.74, 16.83, 16.100. References to Chapter 16 of the Book of Regulations are to the version issued in April 1996

[8] The forthcoming upgrade of the Procurator Fiscal Service Standard Office System will facilitate the provision of such statistics

from nine weeks to almost eight months later. It was unclear whether any of these could have been reported earlier.

Time intervals were calculated in 21 cases for the period between the police report to the procurator fiscal and the first court appearance. Ten cases appeared within a week but the remaining cases first appeared in court from three to 15 months later.

The 11 cases that were completed at court took an average of 23 weeks from first appearance to the first day of the final hearing, ranging from two to 44 weeks.

Taken stage by stage, these figures do not give the full picture of the delays experienced by children in the criminal justice process. At the close of the project, a calculation was made for the 21 cases which had been completed at court or were still pending. These cases had taken an average of 45 weeks from the date on which they were reported to the police to the date of court disposal or, for those that were still pending, to 1 September 1998. However, ten cases had taken over a year and another five had taken between six months and a year. In previous research on child witnesses in Scotland, carers reported that 'the very long delay between reporting the incident and the trial (sometimes as long as a year) was the greatest source of stress for both them and their children'.[9]

It was impossible to tell whether child witness cases had received priority in comparison to prosecutions in general as no statistics are published in Scotland about the pace of sheriff court or High Court cases.

MEDICAL EXAMINATIONS

Children in 12 of the 26 pilot cases were medically examined. Four cases involved physical injuries which were treated at casualty departments. The eight remaining cases involved allegations of sexual assault. The majority were not dealt with according to policy on best practice.

Police surgeons carried out examinations on police premises in five cases; three were conducted by a consultant paediatrician at hospital (two of these were conducted jointly with another hospital physician). Two children in one case were examined twice for forensic purposes, both times by police surgeons. In four cases, police surgeon examinations were conducted some time after the most recent alleged offence, ranging from five weeks to ten months later.

Crown Office policy sets standards for doctors conducting examinations including the expectation that they will be trained in the use of colposcopes.[10] Procurators fiscal were expected to maintain a list of suitable experts and distribute it to the police, reporter and social work department.[11] Joint examinations by forensically trained paediatricians constituted

---

[9] K. Murray (1995) Preparing Child Witnesses for Court. Scottish Office Central Research Unit
[10] Book of Regulations 16.53, 16.56
[11] Book of Regulations 16.51

best practice, with joint examination by a suitably trained police surgeon and paediatrician as a secondary alternative.[12] When the project started, long-standing proposals in Glasgow for joint examinations by paediatricians or by a paediatrician and police surgeon had not been implemented, although joint paediatric – forensic examinations conducted in hospitals had been established in Lothian.[13] Most examinations of children in Glasgow were carried out by police surgeons who did not specialise in child sexual abuse and who had not been trained in the use of colposcopes.[14] This equipment was not available in police examination suites. In the first six months of 1998, a total of 74 child medical examinations were conducted in Greater Glasgow. Fifty-eight per cent of all examinations and 79 per cent of those concerning sexual abuse were carried out in police stations.[15] In England and Wales, forensic examinations of children are no longer carried out in police stations.[16]

A wide range of policies agreed that children should not be subjected to unnecessary medical examination.[17] It is recognised that only a small proportion of forensic examinations result in clinically significant findings.[18] During Phase One, police surgeons acknowledged that they rarely challenged a police request for an examination to be carried out, and their guidance emphasised the need for examinations.[19] Social workers, however, thought that medical examinations were sometimes over-used: 'It's a comfort to the agency, not the child'. As a result of increased inter-agency dialogue, in the Lothian project only 42 per cent of referrals proceeded to medical examinations.

According to policy and good practice, children should be given a choice as to whether the examination is carried out by a male or female doctor.[20] Guidance for police surgeons stated that such requests should be complied with 'unless it is clearly impracticable or would unduly delay the examination'.[21] When this study began, only one female police surgeon was assigned to a police division in Glasgow.

Examinations in five pilot cases were conducted by female doctors who were either police surgeons or paediatricians. One victim to be examined by a police surgeon insisted that the

---

[12] Book of Regulations 16.53

[13] J. Mok et al (1998) The Joint Paediatric – Forensic Examination in Child Abuse. Child Abuse Review Vol. 7:194-203

[14] The Metropolitan Police requires police surgeons handling child abuse cases to undergo a four-day course. A separate two-day course on examination in rape cases is done in conjunction with genito-urinary medical units who see victims who do not report to the police

[15] Figures supplied by Strathclyde Police

[16] Dr Frances Lewington, Metropolitan Police Services

[17] See, for example, Strathclyde Regional Council Child Protection Committee (undated) 7.1; Book of Regulations 16.46 and 16.51; Report of a Working Group set up by the Secretary of State for Scotland and the Lord Advocate (June 1995); Strathclyde Regional Council Department of Education (1993)

[18] See, for example, J. Bays and D. Chadwick (1993): a survey of 21 research reports found that indicators diagnostic of sexual abuse – for example, the presence of genital trauma, sexually transmitted disease or sperm – were found in only three to 16 per cent of child victims

[19] Training for police casualty surgeons, Strathclyde Police Force training (undated)

[20] Book of Regulations 16.53. An information booklet supplied by Victim Support to victims of sexual assault (1995) states that 'most Scottish police forces have female doctors and you have the right to ask for one'

[21] Training for police casualty surgeons, Strathclyde Police Force Training (undated)

examination be carried out by a female doctor. This was arranged, though the examination had to be postponed. In another case in which such a request was made, when the delay was explained the girl agreed to be examined by a male doctor. Her carer said later that he was very gentle with the girl 'but I'm sure she'd have done a lot better if it had been a woman'.

Following the end of the study, procedures for joint examinations in accordance with best practice were introduced in Glasgow.

SUPPORT AND PREPARATION OF YOUNG WITNESSES

PHASE ONE FINDINGS

In 1990, the Scottish Law Commission took the position that young witnesses could give evidence 'by conventional means without suffering undue trauma or stress' provided that they received:

> 'careful pre-trial preparation, in the sense of explaining to the child what to expect, coupled with sensitive handling of the child from the moment of arrival at the court house'.[22]

Phase One of the study therefore examined the provision of support and preparation for young witnesses before court and when they gave evidence, and looked for examples of the sensitive handling and innovative procedures envisaged by the Commission.

Telling children about procedures at court

Fear of the unknown is a major cause of anxiety for child witnesses. To allay such fears, preparation for court should tell children about court procedures in their case. In its 1990 report, the Scottish Law Commission acknowledged the problem of predicting how young witnesses would be dealt with at trial:

> 'where attempts are made, by prosecutors and others, to prepare a child for the experience of giving evidence, it may be difficult to do so accurately and effectively where certain practices and procedures are merely discretionary'.[23]

Without removing this discretion, the Commission hoped that the issuance of judicial guidance would promote 'some desirable uniformity of approach' in judges' treatment of child witnesses. The guidance was issued in 1990 by Lord Hope as the Lord Justice General's Memorandum. The majority of interviewees across the professions in our study considered that the Memorandum had not led to a more consistent judicial approach and it was still impossible to tell young witnesses with any certainty about the measures to be adopted at trial. Implementation of Memorandum procedures is described in detail below. Reporters could request special procedures for young witnesses at children's hearing court proceedings but again, decisions were not made by the sheriff until the day. Wide variations in judicial practice in Glasgow rendered the process unpredictable which in turn caused difficulty in advising children about what to expect. One reporter commented:

> 'It is impossible to prepare a child for proof. We can't tell the child who will be there or where they will sit. The sheriff may object to the support person. Some won't even allow the reporter to escort the child in and out of court'.

---

[22] Para. 1.8
[23] Para. 2.2

In contrast, in a nearby court where the sheriffs' conduct of children's hearing court proceedings was described as 'consistent and sensitive', the reporter felt 'better able to reassure children about what would happen at court'.

The scope of preparation

In both summary and solemn cases, the Crown Office's illustrated leaflet 'Going to Court' aimed at witnesses under 12 was sent out by the procurator fiscal with the citation. It was available only from the fiscal; social workers from the local authority and voluntary organisations were unable to obtain supplies for children they dealt with.

Procurators fiscal offered children familiarisation visits to the court in petition cases only. In summary cases, they were simply advised to meet children on the morning of the trial diet [24] although bringing the child in early to see the courtroom conflicted directly with policy to keep the child at court for as short a time as possible.[25] The aim of the visit was to explain procedures, identify the child's concerns and respond to questions.[26] On occasion, familiarisation visits were also conducted by court-based social workers and court personnel. None of the groups had a standard approach to the way these visits were conducted or the information provided.

The question most frequently asked by children concerned where the accused would be in he courtroom. Some feared that the accused would be free to approach them. Answering these questions was problematic for prosecutors:

> 'Telling the child "I can't tell you where the accused is going to be" is a real legal fiction. It's the child's big issue and we can't address it'.

Some social workers and bar officers were unaware of the need for caution and answered these questions directly:

> 'I take children around the court. They always ask "Will he be here?" I tell them where he will be and where everyone sits' (bar officer).

When screens were used, procurators fiscal had no guidance about what to tell the child regarding the accused's presence on the other side of the screen. One child who had received no explanation asked what her daddy's shoes were doing in court.

During Phase One, Crown Office guidance was revised to reflect that where the accused and the child are well known to one another, the child could be told that the accused would probably be seated in the dock. Where identification was contentious, the child should be told

---

[24] Book of Regulations 16.124. During Phase Two, procurators fiscal began offering pre-trial visits to child witnesses in all summary cases

[25] Book of Regulations 16.100: Where for some pressing reason a case cannot be taken first, special arrangements may be made for the child to attend court at a later time of the day on a 'stand-by' basis

[26] Book of Regulations 16.103, 16.105

that the accused would be in court and the child would be asked to point out the person responsible.[27]

Crown Office guidance emphasised the importance of allowing children to express a view about their preferred evidential option before an application is made. However, a decision about whether an application for CCTV was appropriate was routinely made before the child's familiarisation visit to the court and they were only shown the CCTV if an application had already been made and granted. When the CCTV link was demonstrated on familiarisation visits, children seldom had the opportunity to see the overview of the TV link room on the judge's monitor. Using the link from both ends reassures the child that the judge can always see him or her, even if the child cannot see the judge. Demonstrations of the equipment were often subject to pressure of time. Access to CCTV facilities was between 4 and 5 p.m., at lunchtime or before court started in the morning. Microphones and screens were not set up on pre-trial visits.

The scope of support from different organisations

The Phase One mapping exercise suggested that availability of assistance was determined more by case characteristics than the needs of individual children. Special provisions were targeted at victim witnesses in sexual assault petition cases. However, sexual offences accounted for relatively few young witnesses. Sexual and other offences committed by members of the child's family or someone with care of a child under 16 years old were investigated by specially trained FACU officers[28], sometimes jointly with the social work department. Petition cases involving sexual assault by a family member were likely to be assigned to the procurator fiscal child witness unit, whose personnel developed expertise in these cases. The unit's support efforts concentrated on the precognition interview, seen as an opportunity to answer questions from the child and carer, and the pre-trial familiarisation visit to the court.

Even where some support was provided, there was little continuity of contact for children and families with professionals, with the exception of reporters who often dealt with a case from start to finish. Police FACU officers were expected to establish 'direct contact at the earliest opportunity to ensure physical and psychological support' but this did not extend to support of child witnesses prior to and during court attendance and it was unusual for a FACU officer to escort a child on a pre-trial visit to the court.[29] Cases within the procurator fiscal's office moved laterally through stages in which different personnel were involved. Children could be seen by a safeguarder who prepared a report for a children's hearing, and also by a curator ad litem if the children's hearing referred the matter to a proof hearing in the sheriff court. Curators and safeguarders felt that preparation and support was only a limited part of their role.

---

[27] Book of Regulations 16.105
[28] Strathclyde Police (4 May 1995): indecent exposure, although covered by police child abuse guidelines, was dealt with by uniformed officers in some divisions
[29] Strathclyde Police (July 1994); M. Burman and S. Lloyd (1993) Police Specialist Units for the Investigation of Crimes of Violence against Women and Children in Scotland para. 11.8

Categories of young witnesses less likely to receive a special response included witnesses in summary cases, those who were victims of assaults by persons outside the family and children who were bystanders, not victims themselves. Young witnesses in homicide cases were not dealt with by FACU officers or the procurator fiscal child witness unit. No special provisions were identified for the support of young witnesses from ethnic minorities or those with special needs and few interviewees had any direct experience of such cases in the court system. One senior social worker serving an inner-city area with a significant ethnic minority population had received only one referral in five years. These findings were a concern but it was beyond the scope of our study to explore the reasons for the absence of such cases in the system.

Reporters felt that support was particularly unsatisfactory for children who were not the subject of children's hearing court proceedings:

> 'These children get a very raw deal. We don't give them pre-court visits and we don't support them because we don't have time but this is a pretty poor excuse. No-one thinks about special provisions for them'.

In cases of assault by a stranger or someone outside the extended family, inter-agency policy acknowledged the need to counsel the child victim and family and advised that a social work referral or even compulsory measures of care might be necessary if the parental response was inappropriate or harmful.[30] However, interviewees' thought there was little likelihood of non-familial assaults being referred to the social work department or the reporter during the course of routine police procedures. Case conferences were unlikely to be convened for victims of offences outside the family where there were no immediate child protection issues. The social work department acknowledged that there were many young witnesses in criminal or children's hearing court proceedings for whom it could offer no support.[31]

A Social Worker based at the High Court in Edinburgh had developed particular expertise in arrangements for young witnesses and this contribution was valued by children and professionals alike. When the new High Court building opened in Glasgow in 1997, one social worker began to develop this area of work as part of her overall responsibilities.

Concerns about 'coaching' and misinformation

As one defence advocate has pointed out, the most promising strategy for undermining the child's evidence is to 'exploit the issue of suggestibility', namely that the child's account is the result of talking to adults:

> 'It gives the jury a reason for not believing the child... with the added advantage that it does not necessarily involve accusing the child of deliberately lying...'.[32]

---

[30] Strathclyde Regional Council Child Protection Committee (undated) 2.1; 8.3
[31] Strathclyde Social Work Department (undated)
[32] G. Jackson, QC 'Advocacy Techniques with Children' presentation at the seminar 'Children's Evidence in Court' (14.6.1997) Advocates Criminal Law Group and Advocates Child and Family Law Group, Edinburgh

Police officers, procurators fiscal, reporters, social workers, curators ad litem and safeguarders shared a concern about doing anything to prepare the child for court that could be construed as rehearsing the child's evidence, even though 'the caution exercised by the law enforcement and social work agencies could be felt by children and their parents as indifference and neglect'.[33] Even procurators fiscal were warned that they might be open to the criticism of coaching, even though the Scottish Law Commission doubted whether this was a problem and commented that prosecutors would guard against anything untoward being said to the child prior to trial.[34]

Social work principles included helping children to give evidence in the most effective and least stressful way and supporting their carers. However, workers were warned to avoid compromising themselves, the children or the children's evidence.[35] A strong commitment to further the best interests of the child was undermined by confusion about roles and a feeling that they were unable to protect the child in the criminal or proof process. Criticisms voiced during the Orkney and Ayrshire cases[36] had made social workers apprehensive of pre-court work. None of the social work interviewees felt confident about this area of work and in consequence, best practice for children was perceived as 'by no means standard':

> 'The vast majority of children do not get the necessary support'

> 'It's no-one's responsibility to give support when it's necessary... There is no support formula, only a series of ad hoc arrangements'

> 'We have no guidance on the preparation of a young person to give evidence – there is a desperate need here'

> 'The truth is, we're not clear about what we should be doing, and I don't think anyone else is either'

> 'How do you prepare a child when you don't have the foggiest what will be allowed in terms of support?'.

Voluntary organisations saw their strengths as providing advocacy and counselling which were not available from the social work department. However, they often felt distanced from the court process and the mainstream organisations. Because of the lack of written guidance and training about what constituted appropriate support, they also felt poorly equipped to help parents and children at court. Procurators fiscal had little contact with the social work department or voluntary organisations. Prosecutors and reporters shared a concern about the

---

[33]: K. Murray (1995) Preparing Child Witnesses for Court. Scottish Office Central Research Unit
[34] Book of Regulations 16.105
[35] Strathclyde Social Work Department (8 November 1993)
[36] The Report of the Inquiry into the Removal of Children from Orkney in February 1991. HMSO; L, Petitioners (No 1) 1993 SLT 1310; L, Petitioners (no. 2) 1993 SLT 1342; (IH) 1993 SCLR 693 (sub nom L v Kennedy). An account of both cases can be found in A. Lockyer and F. Stone (1998) Juvenile Justice in Scotland: twenty-five years of the welfare approach. T & T Clark

potential for well-intentioned social workers to misinform children and families because of poor knowledge of the court process.

Reporters were responsible for the presentation of evidence and consideration of the child's competency and ability to withstand cross-examination. This meant they too felt constrained in their support role due to fear of contaminating the child's evidence.

None of the sheriffs or judges interviewed in Phase One expressed concern about familiarisation of the child with the court process. Although there had been objections in certain cases to the way investigative interviews had been conducted, they knew of no instances in which the defence had challenged the child's evidence on the basis of contamination by pre-trial preparation for court.

Informing those responsible for the child about the status of the case

Crown Office policy required parents or guardians to be kept informed about dates of proceedings, special bail conditions, the possibility of defence precognition, the pre-trial court visit and other matters.[37] However, revised policy omitted a previous commitment to give the carer a named contact person at an early stage.[38] In practice, there appeared to be long intervals when carers were unsure about what was happening with the case or about whom to contact. Without a named contact in the procurator fiscal's office, carers and social workers were more likely to approach the police for information. Officers also experienced difficulties in finding out about case status. There was a perception that outside of the child witness unit, there was 'no ownership of cases at the fiscal's office'.

Social workers also complained about the difficulty of obtaining information about case progress, presentation of the child's evidence or who could accompany the child at court. The resulting uncertainty had an adverse impact on preparation of the child:

> 'We liase with the fiscal and reporter to find out what's happening and get back to families by phone. We hardly ever get to the fiscal directly. It's usually a clerk who doesn't know who has got the case'

> 'We are always calling the fiscal's office for information and getting nowhere. Then they are annoyed because we haven't done things right'

> 'You never know what's going on. You wait a while then phone the fiscal's office. They might say "oh, we threw that out five months ago" or, worse, nobody knows anything about it'.

The experience of young witnesses at court

The Phase One study looked at the treatment of child witnesses giving evidence in criminal trials or proof proceedings. In July 1990, the Lord Justice General issued a Memorandum to

---

[37] Book of Regulations 16.76, 16.79
[38] Formerly Book of Regulations 16.62

judges with the objective of ensuring, so far as is reasonably practicable, that the giving of evidence by all children under the age of 16 'causes as little anxiety and distress to the child as possible in the circumstances' while having regard to the court's duty to ensure that the accused receives a fair trial. The Memorandum, which pre-dated legislative provisions for screens and CCTV, gives four examples of measures available at the discretion of the trial judge:

- the removal of wigs and gowns by all participants
- clearing the courtroom
- positioning the child out of the witness box
- permitting a relative or other support person to sit alongside the child.

Four judges and four sheriffs were interviewed. Two said they asked whether the child wanted wigs and gowns removed, but the majority did not remove wigs and gowns routinely:

> 'Children are disappointed if judges are not in fancy dress'

> 'I am in favour of keeping wigs on – it helps set the tone'.

Judges had the power to clear the court when a child was giving evidence and the Memorandum described this as 'normally appropriate' in offences against decency or morality. In other cases it should be done if the judge was satisfied that it was necessary to avoid undue anxiety or distress to the child. Interviewees described this measure as being used frequently in sexual offence cases though not otherwise.

The Memorandum suggested that the child sit at the table in the well of the court along with the judge, counsel and solicitors. Procurators fiscal were advised to ask children what they preferred at the pre-trial meeting or on the morning of trial.[39] Interviewees cited examples of younger children being allowed to give evidence from the well of the court or the bench, but also of children as young as five being required to testify from the witness box. Some judges and sheriffs opted to have the child sit beside them on the bench though it was unclear whether children were asked about this ahead of time. The need to hear a soft-spoken child was emphasised. The provision of a microphone was not routine and even where used, did not always work well. Sheriffs were more willing than judges to come off the bench when young witnesses were in court; only one judge did so. Other judges said:

> 'I can't sit at a busy clerk's table and anyway, it doesn't make a difference'

> 'It may be hard to elicit the truth if I come off the bench, and it is too informal'.

The Memorandum specified that a relative or other person could act as supporter but should not be a witness. Crown Office policy required the procurator fiscal to identify the best

---

[39] Book of Regulations 16.131

person to support the child, usually the parent or carer, bearing in mind the child's wishes.[40] Most judges and sheriffs were open to the use of a supporter though one did not want the person sitting alongside the child as permitted by the Memorandum. Another did not permit the child to be accompanied by a supporter in a jury trial. Judicial views varied as to whether a parent was appropriate in the support role. Sheriffs thought the question should be addressed at a pre-trial diet. Court clerks in High Court cases suggested that where the issue of the support person had not been resolved before the day of trial, contact should be made with the clerk who would alert the judge of the issue before the trial started.

The Memorandum required the judge to warn the supporter not to prompt or seek to influence the child in any way in the course of the evidence. Procurators fiscal were advised to explain the role to the supporter.[41] However, the lack of specific guidance was a concern for social workers and others:

> 'We don't know how to act as a support person at court. Can I touch her if she's upset or say "there, there"? It's hopeless'

> 'I accompanied a nine-year-old who gave evidence for a very long time. I had to sit at the back of the TV link room and could not touch her. At one point she wanted to go to the loo and was told she couldn't. It was just going through the motions to say I was supporting her'.

In Kathleen Murray's study, a supporter accompanied most children giving evidence by CCTV.[42] However, one judge in our study described a case in which a 13-year-old witness who was left by herself in the CCTV room while giving evidence ran out when she became distressed. He felt that the child should not have been on her own. Interviewees told us that in both CCTV and cases in the courtroom, supporters were sometimes disallowed on the day of trial by the judge or sheriff or more commonly, where the person proposed was challenged by the defence at the last minute.[43] One example concerned a stranger assault case in which the defence would not agree that the child's teacher could accompany her in the CCTV room. He consented to the girl being accompanied by a social worker who had not met the girl before, although he was reluctant to let the social worker be introduced to her beforehand. In such instances, Kathleen Murray found that:

> 'The resulting confusion and interruption to the timetable caused upset and worry to the children, precisely at the moment when they needed to keep calm'.[44]

---

[40] Book of Regulations 16.108
[41] Book of Regulations 16.108
[42] Kathleen Murray's research identified only one out of 49 children giving evidence by TV link who did not have a support person present; 84% of supporters were well known to the child (1995)paras. 10.6-7
[43] Procurators fiscal are advised to seek the defence's agreement to avoid having to obtain someone else at the eleventh hour. If objection seems likely, contingency arrangements should be made: Book of Regulations 16.108
[44] (1995) para. 10.8

Supporters interviewed by Kathleen Murray felt that the restrictions on their role in the TV link room were unreasonable. She recommended that supporters should receive written guidance and be able to alert the judge if technical or other problems arose for the child while giving evidence.[45]

The Lord Justice General's Memorandum was not intended to confine the exercise of a judge's discretion to the four procedures provided as examples. Judges and sheriffs described other measures to make the child feel more comfortable:

- allowing a child to write down what had happened to her so that she could answer questions about it
- asking children to speak slowly and explaining that everything is being written down
- telling children ahead of time that it is alright to say 'I don't know' or 'I can't remember' and reminding them of this at the start of their testimony
- asking children to say if they need the toilet: 'I ask them how they would attract their teacher's attention and tell them to put their hand up'
- making sure they have a drink: 'Kids dehydrate if under pressure'
- saying 'thank you' at the end of children's testimony.

A few sheriffs introduced themselves to the child before the trial started and judges and sheriffs generally favoured the prosecutor doing so. However, some advocates depute refused to do so despite being requested to meet young witnesses by procurators fiscal.

The statutory options: screens, CCTV and evidence on commission

An application for one of the statutory options was appropriate only 'in exceptional cases', with screens preferred over CCTV and evidence on commission considered only where neither of the other options was suitable.[46] It was theoretically possible to make successive applications; for example where the judge refused an application for screens an application for CCTV could be made, but interviewees in our study had never seen this done. The provisions for evidence on commission allow the child's evidence to be taken before a commissioner and video-recorded, with the video-recording to be shown at trial. The application can only be made once the witness has been cited to give evidence. No child witness had given evidence on commission in Scotland and interviewees throughout this study did not envisage circumstances in which it would be used in the near future.

Screens could be used to block eye contact between the child witness and the accused. Sometimes a small camera was positioned so that the accused could see the child on a monitor. The use of the camera was not always explained by the fiscal before the trial. Because children were not shown the screens and camera on the pre-trial court visit, those supporting young witnesses were concerned that a child noticing the camera in court for the first time while giving evidence could be disconcerted or even distressed.

---

[45] (1995) para. 10.16, recommendations p. 151
[46] Book of Regulations 16.121

Interviewees identified a range of problems concerning the use of CCTV:

> 'Judges don't understand, either because of the size of the little screen which shows what the child sees, or because the judge is taking notes and not looking, that what the child sees over the link is a "looming" face or just the top of an advocate's head' (procurator fiscal)[47]

> 'The judge should not just turn off the TV link without explaining to the child first' (procurator fiscal)

> 'Sheriffs have very mixed views about CCTV. The ones who don't like it are the ones who don't know how to use it' (sheriff)

> 'Counsel may talk to the screen, not to the camera. Sheriffs are usually taking a note and don't look at the screen' (procurator fiscal)

> 'The defence will say "Do you know daddy is listening to this?" which is abusive as the whole purpose is for the child not to be reminded about the presence of the accused' (social worker)[48].

Only three of the eight judicial interviewees had experience with CCTV. One mentioned the difficulty of holding the child's attention. Another referred to a case in which an application for CCTV had been granted but, due to pressure of business, the trial was moved to another court with no facilities. He said the children had testified perfectly well:

> 'I prefer children to give evidence in open court. Their candour can be so devastating'.

On the morning of trial, court personnel often take the judge through the operation of the equipment. There was no written guidance for the judiciary to follow when the TV link was used. Some judicial interviewees thought a 'ready reference' of this type, which could include suggested jury instructions, would be helpful (see Annex A).

Judicial intervention

Many interviewees were troubled about questioning of children perceived as oppressive or, more commonly, developmentally inappropriate. Procurator fiscal policy acknowledged that a witness must be able to understand the questions which should be framed simply and that use of terms and expressions familiar to the child will help understanding.[49] Experienced defence solicitors agreed that good practice required the use of simple language and short sentences appropriate to the child's developmental, not chronological, age.[50]

---

[47] Fiscals are reminded to object if such practices are adopted: Book of Regulations 16.112
[48] This should also be the subject of an objection: Book of Regulations 16.112
[49] Book of Regulations 16.68; 16.132
[50] Karen Saywitz, an American expert in child witness evidence, recommends counting the number of words and syllables in the child's sentences and using this as one measure of what constitutes an appropriate question

Judicial interviewees varied in the extent to which they felt able to intervene in inappropriate questioning:

> 'We are handicapped because we are not inquisitors'

> 'It is not for me to be too interventionist'

> 'I will stop someone tripping up the child. If the question is too long I will say something before the child has to'

> 'I would intervene if a child was distressed or if questions used inappropriate vocabulary. I would ask counsel to rephrase or I have no compunction to paraphrase if it is clear that the child does not understand'

> 'I would intervene if the child was at risk of being distressed or of not understanding questions'.

Interviewees singled out some members of the judiciary for their thoughtful treatment of children but thought that others did not intervene even if the child was being badgered or asked repetitive questions. Procurators fiscal, reporters and curators identified instances of judicial behaviour which fell outside the 'sensitive handling of the child' envisaged by the Scottish Law Commission:

> 'I have been refused permission to have a support person for an eight-year-old. The sheriff said "I went to boarding school when I was eight and he can certainly come into court on his own". Another sheriff stopped someone holding a young child's hand while coming into court'

> 'A child psychologist gave evidence about a 15-year-old girl who had been abused. The sheriff said that he did not care about this evidence and called the girl a "lying little bitch". She was present in the hearing'

> 'I once took three children to Sheriff X's court before the hearing. I let them sit in his chair on the bench. They were very soft spoken and I wanted them to see that it was high up and they would need to speak up later when giving evidence. The sheriff came in and was furious, demanding to know what was happening. I explained that it was an approved visit but the children were terrified'.

Procurators fiscal, reporters and curators often felt unable to intervene in court on behalf of a child witness:

> 'The sheriff asked a seven-year-old to put her hand down her pants and show where the man touched her. Then he asked her to do it again. No-one intervened. We can't object – it's the sheriff's court'

> 'When the sheriff behaves inappropriately, pragmatism may demand that we do nothing. It is very important that we learn to deal with this'

> 'I used to say to children "It's my job to keep you safe" – I soon gave that up!'

> 'The whole court scenario is awful. There is so much aggression and tension that you are reluctant to interfere. There is a huge need for better management'

> 'I don't know if we can intervene. I wouldn't dare with a senior sheriff'.

The competency test

Judges and sheriffs mentioned difficulties in assessing children's competence and thought that practical guidance on age-appropriate questions would be useful.[51] Several indicated that they found the whole process artificial and said they had no confidence in the responses:

> 'The competency test is a shibboleth but it can go badly wrong if it is done in an adult fashion'.

Before hearsay evidence can be admitted in proof hearings, the sheriff must be satisfied about the competency of the child making the original statement as well as the competency and accuracy of the person giving the 'hearsay' evidence to the court. A solicitor provided an example of the problems caused by the requirement to examine the competency of the child in this situation:

> 'The child (aged five) had been interviewed extensively by the social work department… I felt that the child should be led in evidence only so far as it would allow the sheriff to establish her competency and thereafter the intention was to rely on the child's hearsay evidence as given by the interviewer. The father's representatives, however, took the view that once a child started to give evidence then she could be questioned about any matter relevant to the case. It is not surprising therefore that the child broke down after only a very short period under cross-examination. I believe that there must be some method of independently assessing the child's credibility and reliability which will be acceptable to all parties in the judicial process'.

In 1997, the Scottish Courts Administration conducted a consultation exercise on the competency test. It has indicated that in due course it plans to conduct a further consultation

---

[51] Extracts from 'Handbook on Questioning Children' (1994) American Bar AssociationCenter on Children and the Law, were supplied to the Director of Judicial Studies in Scotland at his request

exercise on the compellability of children. When this is completed, a package of reforms relating to children's evidence may be taken forward.[52]

Post-proceedings support

Crown Office policy was clear that, where children and their carers wish to be informed of the case outcome, the procurator fiscal should see or contact them as soon as possible after the trial is concluded.[53] However, due to pressure of work fiscals found it difficult to follow up as quickly as they would have liked:

> 'Sometimes families find out about the verdict from the newspaper. This responsibility should lie with the fiscal – we have a moral responsibility for younger witnesses'.

Police officers who were not witnesses were unable to pass on information about case outcomes to children and families unless they themselves had been told the result by the procurator fiscal. Social workers also commented that their ability to provide post-court support was curtailed by the difficulty of obtaining information about what had happened at court or how decisions were reached.[54]

The role of a child witness supporter

The Scottish Law Commission had considered the appointment of someone to protect and perhaps represent the interests of a child witness in criminal proceedings:

> 'to provide a measure of continuous support for the child right up to, and including, the proceedings in court, and enable the child to be better prepared for the giving of evidence than might otherwise be the case'.

Although the majority of those consulted by the Commission agreed that it would be desirable to have someone look after the child's interests both before and during the trial, some questioned the desirability of creating a new position for this purpose. The Commission therefore made no specific recommendation but concluded that:

> 'under existing arrangements, it may be possible for those concerned – prosecutors, social workers, safeguarders and others – to consider and develop new and improved ways to protect the child's interests, *and we urge them to do so*' (emphasis added).[55]

Our study found little evidence of the innovative procedures envisaged by the Commission. At the end of Phase One, the Working Group concluded that a child witness officer (CWO)

---

[52] Consultation Paper on Further Measures to Support Child Witnesses in Civil and Criminal Proceedings (1997) Scottish Courts Administration; letter from the Scottish Courts Administration, 24.7.98
[53] Book of Regulations 16.137(a)
[54] Strathclyde Social Work Department (undated); Strathclyde Social Work Department (4 May 1995)
[55] Para. 5.4

should be appointed on an experimental basis during the pilots. The responsibilities of the CWO would include:

- developing a protocol on the preparation of child witnesses
- acting as a central information point and facilitating preparation carried out by others
- acting as a 'safety net' by preparing some children for court who would not otherwise receive this service
- providing feedback to the Working Group about compliance with policy commitments and the experience of children and families at court.

It was envisaged that the CWO would develop a body of knowledge which would enable training to be provided to others preparing children for court, leading eventually to the support function being assigned to a designated, trained group.

PHASE TWO

The Support and preparation Pilot

The support and preparation subgroup was initially chaired by Glasgow Social Work Department and subsequently by Victim Support. Members represented the Strathclyde Police, Procurator Fiscal Service, Scottish Court Service and the Law Society of Scotland. In February 1997, Ouainé Bain, a child psychologist, was appointed as CWO for a period of one year in a part-time position funded by NCH Action for Children and Children 1st. She attended meetings of this and other pilot subgroups and provided status reports about her work at Working Group meetings.

The subgroup agreed five key principles to be observed by those engaged in the preparation of young witnesses for court:

> **Key principles for the preparation of child witnesses**
>
> - there must be no discussion of the child's evidence or the circumstances of the alleged offence
>
> - while taking care that preparation does not compromise the judicial process and the interests of justice, the welfare of the child witness is a paramount consideration
>
> - the needs of the individual child should be taken into consideration as far as possible
>
> - those preparing the child must work in partnership with other agencies and take account of different professional perspectives
>
> - those preparing the child must work in partnership with non-abusing parents and carers and inform them of their rights and obligations within the court process.

The objectives of the support and preparation pilot were:

- to provide direct support, assistance and information to child witnesses
- to help them develop appropriate skills which would allow them to testify as fully as possible
- to create an opportunity for them to feel empowered by the experience of giving evidence
- to provide support and information to carers, assisting them to support children appropriately
- to help the child and family cope with the stress and anxiety associated with the witness role
- to communicate information about the child to others in the court process with the aim of ensuring that treatment of the child is appropriate to his or her needs and abilities.

One initial objective, 'to assist the child in achieving as complete a recall of information as possible' was dropped because refreshing the recollection of a witness before trial by reviewing previous statements was not permissible.

The subgroup also established objectives for the evaluation of the CWO position in order to assess its impact:

- to improve services to children and families in the pre-trial and court process
- to facilitate the flow of information in individual cases
- to raise awareness of good practice generally.

Eight cases were referred to the CWO at a point when it seemed likely that a child would be required to give evidence. In two, the CWO did not have contact with the children. The procurator fiscal decided not to call the children as witnesses in one case before the CWO had done other than make basic enquiries. In the other, the parents declined the CWO's offer of help but the police asked for the CWO's advice and she went on to advise the precognoscer. That child was an eye-witness in a murder trial and the police were concerned because her parents had not wanted her to cooperate with the prosecution.

Of the eight referrals, two were summary and six involved solemn proceedings. Four involved sexual offences. By the end of the CWO's tenure, the High Court murder case and one summary case had ended in trials; three sheriff court cases had resulted in guilty pleas and one had been discontinued. One High Court and one sheriff court case were still pending and arrangements were made for someone else to support the children at trial in these cases.

The CWO's position was part-time. Although she was available to take referrals from April 1997, she did not begin to receive referrals until September 1997. In the interim, her time was used to develop the project protocol and other child witness materials, in assisting the work of the other pilot subgroups and in conducting briefings and establishing contacts with others working with young witnesses.

Support and preparation pilot objectives: to provide direct support, assistance and information to child witnesses; to help them develop appropriate skills which would allow them to testify as fully as possible; and to create an opportunity for them to feel empowered by the experience of giving evidence

The first task of the subgroup and the CWO was to decide what constituted appropriate support and preparation. Initial discussions focused on relevant research which suggested that simply providing explanations about people's roles at court and giving a tour of the courtroom (the optimum help on offer) was likely to be inadequate to meet children's needs at court and stop them from 'freezing up' when giving evidence. Reference was made to comprehensive preparation programmes which could reduce stress and result in more effective testimony. These aimed to improve the child's:

- complete and accurate recall of information
- understanding of questions and ability to indicate non-comprehension and resist compliance with leading questions
- ability to cope with anxiety
- understanding of trial procedures.[56]

Discussions with interviewees during Phase One had been used to identify activities, both direct (e.g. explaining why a witness must tell the truth) and indirect (e.g. finding out about the child's needs and passing on this information) which were thought not to contaminate children's evidence. The CWO used these lists and the relevant research to develop a

---

[56] J. Spencer and R. Flin (1993) p. 378; K. Sisterman Keeney et al. 'The Court Prep Group: A Vital part of the Court Process' in Children as Witnesses, H. Dent and R. Flin (eds) 1992 John Wiley and Sons; L. Sas et al. (1991)'Reducing the System-Induced Trauma for Child Sexual Abuse Victims through Court Preparation, Assessment and Follow-Up' London Family Court Clinic, Ontario, Canada; J. Aldridge and K. Freshwater (1993) 'The Preparation of Child Witnesses' in Journal of Child Law, Vol. 5, No. 1, pp. 25-26

protocol setting out a detailed support and preparation programme and listing resources, techniques and materials. The protocol emphasised the need to tailor the preparation programme to the needs of the child and the case. This guidance was not just for the CWO but for the eventual use of all those working with young witnesses. The subgroup oversaw the development of this document and the final draft was distributed widely for comment to various groups including sheriffs.

Children under stress needed extra help to absorb information. The research considered by the subgroup had emphasised that children who were given the opportunity to practise question-and-answer techniques were better able to respond appropriately and identify questions they did not understand than those who were only given advice such as 'If you really can't remember what happened, just say that you can't remember'.[57] Initial concerns had been expressed by the procurator fiscal about the use of role play in developing children's ability to cope with questioning. The protocol contained detailed advice on this matter and set out the boundaries of appropriate preparation. When it was distributed for consultation, no concerns about possible contamination were raised concerning the activities described.

Before making contact with the child and carer, the CWO obtained basic information about the child, home circumstances and the case, though not the details of the evidence. She discussed with the police and social worker (if there was one) how she should be introduced. Much of the CWO's work was conducted in the child's home. Parents and siblings were usually involved but if there were too many disruptions, additional meetings with children took place at her office or at their school. Time spent on referrals varied from two to 19 hours per child. This included pre-trial visits, accompanying child witnesses at trial and work after cases had finished.

Sessions began with an explanation to parents and children about the CWO's independent role and that she would not discuss their evidence. If any child had subsequently raised an evidential matter, this would have been referred to the procurator fiscal for an answer, in accordance with the protocol but in the event this did not arise. In one case, the CWO worked jointly with the family social worker who described the mother as 'very vulnerable, agitated and not good at meeting new people'.

Time was taken to discuss children's interests before going on to identify their worries and misapprehensions about court. The principal anxiety shared by the children related to seeing the accused. This concern was not just about court but also 'Where is he now'? Although bail conditions prohibited contact with witnesses, some young witnesses reported seeing the accused on the street in their neighbourhood. The police were not always told of such encounters; one girl who was very upset by this had been reluctant to tell her parents for fear of provoking their anxieties.

A range of materials, some of which the child could keep, was used to explain about what happened at court. Resources included Crown Office booklets for children, an illustrated

---

[57] *Going to Court as a Witness?* Crown Office and Procurator Fiscal Service (1998)

leaflet with pictures of Glasgow Sheriff Court, the NSPCC Child Witness Pack, a model courtroom and a booklet developed by the CWO offering multiple-choice answers to 'what if' questions. Children could choose which materials to 'revisit' with the CWO in subsequent sessions. Some children were also given a notebook in which to write down questions or thoughts about being a witness.

The CWO checked the children's understanding of court 'rules'. Depending on the child's developmental age this was done by playing question and answer games, for example helping children identify questions they could not understand and to say so. In the only case in this pilot to go to trial, both children were able to demonstrate something of what they had learned during these exercises. During a long cross-examination, one autistic boy aged 12 asked the defence to repeat a question and said when he did not know an answer. However, when the cross-examination became harassing in the view of the CWO and researcher, the child became confused and broke down. There were frequent legal debates at the trial which necessitated the children leaving the courtroom. The CWO observed that such incidents need to be explained in pre-trial preparation so that children understood they were not being excluded because they had done something wrong.

After the trial, the autistic boy said that having the CWO 'helped me go to court and made it easier for me'. The other witness in this trial, a girl of 13, said that she had enjoyed her time with the CWO and found her very helpful. However, she had not expected cross-examination to be so bad and her advice to other children would be not to go to court. Nevertheless, her headmaster felt that, despite the stress she had experienced in cross-examination, she had 'come out of her shell' after the trial when she learned that the sheriff had believed her account and 'somehow seemed empowered that she had managed well at court'. In this case, the procurator fiscal had not thought it appropriate to write to the children directly, and asked the CWO to let them know about the trial outcome.

The remaining pilot cases were still pending or had ended in a guilty plea so it was hard to assess the extent to which other children had felt empowered by working with the CWO. Nevertheless, the feedback was positive; for example, a social worker who had observed sessions thought that boys of eight and 11 had found the preparation sessions helpful and fun. He considered that they would probably have coped quite well at court. Their mother said it had helped make the boys less nervous. One became 'quite confident'. The other, who had brain damage, 'always listened carefully when the CWO explained how it would be' but the mother feared he would still have been confused by cross-examination. She said that her sons 'were almost disappointed when they were told they didn't have to go to court'.

Post-court work and debriefing of young witnesses and carers were important, even where cases had not gone to trial. In one case the children decided to visit the court after a guilty plea had been entered. It was felt to be a useful 'closure' and helped them understand how the case had been dealt with. Children were pleased to receive letters from the CWO and the procurator fiscal when the case was over. (In other pilot cases, the researchers were able to pass on to children positive comments about their evidence that had been made by procurators fiscal or sheriffs and this was much appreciated.)

In one pilot case, two children were in care in separate facilities. The CWO played an important role in bridging a communication gap between the care homes and other agencies. This case was discontinued before trial. The procurator fiscal sent letters to the children with a cover letter to their carers asking them to explain to the children that the case would not go to court. The social worker told the carers that she would explain the fiscal's decision to the children but failed to do so. The children had difficulty understanding the legal language of the procurator fiscal's letter. In the end, the CWO took time to ensure that the children understood what had happened.

Support and preparation pilot objectives: to provide support and information to carers, assisting them to support children appropriately and to help the child and family cope with the stress and anxiety associated with the witness role

The pilot subgroup oversaw the development of a booklet for parents, foster carers and people accompanying a young witness to court in criminal proceedings. Five thousand copies of this booklet, 'Your Child is a Witness', were published by Strathclyde Police, with local inserts listing useful organisations. Feedback from carers in pilot cases was positive. For example, one carer used the booklet to prepare a list of questions for the procurator fiscal at precognition. She brought someone with her to act as a supporter for the children, because the booklet explained that as she was a witness herself, she could not act as their supporter. Victim Support began an evaluation of the booklet and initial responses indicated that it was helpful in enabling parents to support their children.

The CWO provided procedural explanations to carers and acted as a liaison for information on case progress. This support was described as valuable by the carers themselves, by the police, procurators fiscal and by social workers who felt that carers were too often overlooked as a resource to support the child.

In addition to factual information, many carers and children were in need of emotional support. The CWO found that the forthcoming trial was frequently only one of several stressful events in their lives, so that support for the child was not necessarily the carers' highest priority. An additional complication reported by carers was that they and their children sometimes concealed their feelings about court in order to protect one another. The intervention of the CWO gave both parents and children someone to talk to. One mother described her son's 'bravado' in talking to her about court but said he was more open and comfortable in sharing his fears with the CWO. Another mother said she was grateful to the CWO because 'I felt too nervous to be much good to the boys.' There were tensions for the children between 'trying to forget about it for a while' and fear of not remembering their evidence at court. Some children voiced anxiety about court outcomes and what would happen if, in the words of one child, 'the judge says innocent'.

The CWO described one aspect of her role as problematic. She acted as courtroom supporter to both children in the only pilot case that went to trial. For reasons that had not been planned, the children gave evidence on different days which meant that after the first child testified, the CWO felt unable to speak to the second child at what his mother described as a 'crucial time when he really needed to'. After the case was completed, a procurator fiscal commented that the CWO could have spoken to the second child before he gave evidence provided that there was no discussion of either child's evidence.

The mother of one of these children criticised the constraints on the support role:

> 'In court, a supporter should be able to give the child a tissue or hold a hand. They weren't even close together! My child was being horrendously abused and the "supporter" had to just sit there. Why on earth do they call it support?'

The mother was not critical of the CWO's behaviour but felt that the procurator fiscal and the sheriff should have intervened in the cross-examination on the child's behalf. She said she was grateful that the CWO had been there; she herself had been too upset and had to leave the court.

Interviewees had been concerned about the lack of guidance on the role of the person accompanying the child while giving evidence. Instructions for these supporters were included in the pilot protocol, with the intention that they could be made available for general use. The guidance covered those accompanying the child in the CCTV room and in the courtroom. Following a recommendation in Kathleen Murray's CCTV evaluation[58], the subgroup discussed whether there were circumstances in which the supporter could intervene to attract the attention of the sheriff or judge, for example when the child was very distressed or when there was a technical problem. The advice of the sheriff and procurator fiscal to the subgroup was that intervention was the responsibility of the sheriff and intervention by the supporter should not be necessary. The guidance therefore reflected that it was up to the procurator fiscal or reporter to raise this matter with the court. If the presiding sheriff agreed, the supporter could use a pre-arranged signal to intervene, but only in 'exceptional circumstances'. The guidance for supporters was developed at a late stage of the pilot and there was no opportunity to test its usefulness.

Support and preparation pilot objective: to communicate information about the child to others in the court process with the aim of ensuring that treatment of the child is appropriate to his or her needs and abilities

Information communicated by the CWO to the procurator fiscal about the children's needs included:

- the children's preferences about how to give evidence and procedures at court (for example, the child's wish, as written in his diary, that he wanted the judge to wear his 'everyday clothes' not a wig and gown)
- conflicts with possible trial dates and other disruptive events in the children's lives, such as moving house and changing school

---

[58] Live Television Link: An Evaluation of its Use by Child Witnesses in Scottish Criminal Trials (1997) Scottish Office Central Research Unit

- discussions with precognoscers about a child with a communication problem, and about advance planning for court
- providing reports about children with learning difficulties.

The CWO was instrumental in other ways, for example:

- alerting the procurator fiscal's attention to information about child witnesses held by the police of which the procurator fiscal was unaware
- requesting the social worker to prepare a report for the procurator fiscal about how the child communicated at the investigative interview
- informing the procurator fiscal of a relevant psychological report held by the social work department and about teachers' views on the children's abilities
- advising the defence precognition agent that the mother had a speech impediment and had difficulty talking on the phone
- telling the procurator fiscal about members of the family that the child did not want in the courtroom
- discussing with the social worker the choice of a supporter outside the family where the children might have had a problem speaking up in front of their carers.

COMMUNICATION OF INFORMATION ABOUT YOUNG WITNESSES WITHIN THE JUSTICE SYSTEM

PHASE ONE FINDINGS

Phase One of the research called for a mapping exercise to describe inter-agency consultation and communication of information about child witnesses. This did not involve evidence in the legal sense but the gathering and passing on of background information about the needs, views and capabilities of the individual child. The justice system cannot respond effectively to the needs of young witnesses without such information.

Policies on inter-agency communication

Inter-agency cooperation in the interests of the child[59] was strongly endorsed in a wide range of policy documents, stressing, for example:

- the avoidance of duplicative interviews and medical examinations[60]
- a structured investigative approach in which decisions were based on consultation[61]
- informing the procurator fiscal and reporter of planned arrangements and inviting them to participate[62]
- earlier and greater involvement by the procurator fiscal than normal[63]
- liaison about the timing of criminal and reporter proceedings[64]
- a readily identifiable contact in each office to deal with information flowing to and from different agencies and allow effective liaison from the outset of a case[65]
- local procedures setting out arrangements for responding to and sharing information about allegations of child abuse, which should include access to specialist advice or expertise.[66]

Agencies emphasised their responsibilities both to communicate information and seek it where it had not been provided. For example, procurators fiscal were advised to:

- obtain information from the police, social worker or carer prior to any precognition

---

[59] Book of Regulations 16.42; see also Protecting Children - A Shared Responsibility (1998) published by the Scottish Office after the end of the study
[60] For example, Book of Regulations 16.44-50 and Annex 4; Strathclyde Regional Council Child Protection Committee (undated) 8.2
[61] For example, Strathclyde Police (June 1993)
[62] 'When Children Speak...' Draft Report of a Working Group set up by the Secretary of State for Scotland and the Lord Advocate (June 1995)
[63] Book of Regulations 16.44
[64] Book of Regulations, Annex 4
[65] Book of Regulations 16.45
[66] Protecting Children - A Shared Responsibility (1998) Scottish Office, p. 19

- assess the child's competence, ability to communicate (with aids if necessary), personality, maturity and the extent of the child's fear of or affection for the accused, and to pass on this 'crucial' information if the precognoscer is not the prosecutor at trial
- take steps to reduce the child's distress and anxiety at trial according to the age and maturity of the individual witness.[67]

Inter-agency communication in practice

Prosecutors emphasised the value of background information:

> 'It can make all the difference in the world to have some special information – how to question the child in a particular way, details from the carer or the police viewpoint or whether there is a "trigger" which will help the child tell her story'.

However, where information about the child was not provided some prosecutors did not have time to request it:

> 'It is always useful to have information about the child but we don't have time to go back and ask'

> 'We already delay to remedy evidential deficiencies. We have not got time to get "nice-to-know" information'.

Some police officers were unaware that in summary proceedings, prosecutors did not meet children before the trial diet because they did not routinely precognosce or (as was the case throughout most of the project) offer familiarisation visits to the court. The police therefore did not appreciate the special need to pass on information about the child to the procurator fiscal in summary cases.

Reporters and procurators fiscal were generally unaware of the official point of contact in the other organisation. Despite some joint training, there was little consensus on good practice in the interaction of these organisations. Reporters said that, on occasion, the procurator fiscal directed that there should be no further interviews with the child. Although this was not binding on reporters, they saw it as a misunderstanding of their role. They were concerned that prosecutors sometimes failed to take account of child protection issues and that the police referred requests from reporters for access to productions to the procurator fiscal for approval in the belief that the fiscal 'owned' the investigation. Reporters' access to subject sheets, copies of charges and statements was said to depend on the quality of the relationship between the individuals involved.

Reporters were concerned about difficulties in obtaining access to evidence in the criminal case. Section 46 of the Children (Scotland) Act 1995 stated that evidence obtained by the procurator fiscal may be supplied to the reporter and used to assist the sheriff in determining an application to establish grounds of referral. The procurator fiscal has the discretion to

---

[67] Book of Regulations 16.43; 16.87-88; 16.94; 16.123; 16.124

refuse to comply with such a request where he reasonably believes that it is necessary to retain the evidence for the purposes of criminal proceedings. According to Crown Office policy, difficulties may arise where the information requested is regarded by the procurator fiscal as confidential or was obtained in pursuance of a criminal investigation warrant. In such circumstances, the instructions of Crown Counsel should be sought.[68]

Children's hearing court proceedings often took place before the criminal trial and where this occurred, the reporter was expected to inform the procurator fiscal about the outcome or any other relevant aspect of the proof.[69] However, where the trial preceded the proof and resulted in a conviction, the prosecutor could ask the criminal court to remit as the grounds are established. Reporters identified several cases in which this had not happened and, as a result, grounds had to be drawn up for a proof hearing in the sheriff court which could otherwise have been avoided. Reporters described occasional tensions with fiscals about the order of proceedings:

> 'It is a big bugbear that the criminal case has priority over care and protection cases'.

Mechanisms for communicating information about the child witness

Procedures for inter-agency communication of information about child witnesses were ad hoc. This was so even concerning children who were the subject of applications for screens or CCTV, for which reports were sought by the procurator fiscal. Such applications and those for evidence on commission could be granted by the court on cause shown. The court can take into account include the age and maturity of the child but must have regard to:

- the possible effect on the child if required to give evidence, if no application is granted
- whether the child would be better able to give evidence if the application is granted
- the child's views.[70]

When the police reporting officer thought that young witnesses fell within the statutory criteria, it was essential that reports to the procurator fiscal contained 'full information' about the children, particularly in relation to the above criteria, so that procurators fiscal could consider 'at an early stage' whether applications should be made.[71] Despite this, police reports rarely included an assessment of the child's abilities or needs. Officers said that their reports did not deal with how the child might give evidence 'because we don't know if the fiscal will take up the case' and because such decisions were not 'their particular remit'.

The procurator fiscal had responsibility to recommend whether an application for CCTV or screens should be made. The application had to be supported by full information about the child's ability to give evidence, the child's views and any other factors which would assist the court. When petition cases were reported to the Crown Office, Crown Counsel marked up the

---

[68] Book of Regulations 16.60
[69] J. Harris and L. Higson (1995)
[70] Criminal Procedure (Scotland) Act 1995, section 271(7) and (8)
[71] Guidelines issued by the Lord Advocate to Chief Constables on the provisions relating to children's evidence in section 271 of the Criminal Procedure (Scotland) Act 1995

case papers in deciding whether applications should be made. Procurators fiscal did not know to what extent Crown Counsel were influenced by the child's preference. Fiscals felt that the main difficulty in putting forward an application lay with convincing advocates depute who took a 'harder line' and sometimes turned down their recommendation that CCTV was necessary, or instituted an application for screens instead. Some advocates depute were also reluctant to meet the child before the start of trial and did not wish the child to be accompanied by a supporter. These attitudes led some procurators fiscal to prefer certain sensitive child witness cases to be dealt with in the sheriff court rather than the High Court.

Supporting reports were routinely obtained from social workers, teachers, doctors, psychiatrists and psychologists, who were asked to address specific questions about the legislative criteria to be satisfied in granting an application.[72] Interviewees who had prepared reports in support of applications believed that they were writing for the trial judge. In High Court cases, applications were dealt with before the trial at a hearing conducted by the Lord Justice Clerk. The supporting reports considered by the Lord Justice Clerk were not provided to the trial judge.

Social workers and voluntary organisations expressed frustration about the difficulty of communicating children's needs to justice system personnel. There was a particular problem for young witnesses of offences committed outside the family who fell outside the terms of reference for social work assistance. Even where children had witnessed a homicide they were not seen as vulnerable witnesses.

There was confusion over agency responsibilities and boundaries in relation to therapy, with a general belief that it was often withheld in case it caused the child's evidence to be challenged at court. Useful guidance produced by NCH Action for Children and counselling projects in Drumchapel and Easterhouse had not been able to overcome practitioners' anxieties.

Crown Office guidance stated that decisions about counselling were the responsibility of the child's carers. The procurator fiscal could only advise whether counselling was likely to have an adverse effect on the prosecution.[73] The question of therapy was not addressed in guidance for reporters and several found the question problematic, saying that they would 'prefer it not to happen in case it clouded the issues at proof' or that 'we don't allow it because the case would be lost if therapy took place'.

Social work guidance warned that however much care was taken when preparing a child, fears about contamination would be raised and workers should be prepared to testify about their work.[74] Counselling should not begin until the social worker liaised with the procurator fiscal and the reporter. Social workers said that the needs of children did not 'sit easily with the demands of the legal system'. They felt unable to challenge what they saw as prohibitions

---

[72] Book of Regulations 16.116
[73] Book of Regulations 16.59
[74] Strathclyde Social Work Department (22 March 1995); (4 May 1995); Strathclyde Regional Council Child Protection Committee (undated) 9.2

on therapy. One voluntary sector social worker reported being told by a procurator fiscal that 'counselling obviously couldn't start until after the court case'. Another social worker had been told by a prosecutor that work focusing on self-protection, not evidence, was not acceptable pre-trial. She commented:

> 'There are a lot of myths about what therapy is. It's not talking about the evidence. We say to children "You don't need to tell us about what happened, and if you are going to court we won't be able to talk about it". Our scheme has not been challenged'.

The Lord Justice General's Memorandum

In July 1990, the Lord Justice General issued a Memorandum to judges with the aim of ensuring that the giving of evidence by all children under the age of 16 caused 'as little anxiety and distress to the child as possible in the circumstances' while having regard to the court's duty to ensure that the accused received a fair trial. The Memorandum asked judges to take each child's particular circumstances into account before deciding what steps, if any, should be taken to minimise anxiety or distress. A number of cases were brought to the project's attention in which basic information about the child had not been communicated to the court, for example, that the child had learning difficulties or had a hearing problem. In one case, a boy with a severe speech impediment was permitted to write answers to questions on a flipchart in the courtroom, but this was only arranged on the morning of the trial.

In Phase One of the research, the Memorandum was discussed with four judges and four sheriffs.[75] Most had relatively little experience with children's evidence. There was no formal mechanism for judges and sheriffs to share information about one another's practice or to receive feedback about problems in individual cases. Some saw the Memorandum, at least in part, as an encroachment on judicial independence:

> 'I don't like directions telling me what to do'

> 'Judges need to have total control of the proceedings'

> 'Perhaps we could do more to standardise – I see the need to make things more predictable for children – but this must be done without tying the hands of judges'.

Judges and sheriffs were often assigned to cases at the last minute, without prior notice that a child witness was involved. Even the most basic information – the age of the child – was not routinely communicated to the judiciary. They said that the child's age was not necessarily on the papers or provided by the prosecution. One said 'We are told nothing' and speculated whether prosecutors were aware of the Memorandum. Another said:

> 'The fiscal should not be telling me there's a young witness as the child comes in. I have had that experience'.

---

[75] The range of views were similar to those of eight sheriffs interviewed in Phase Two

Clerks in the High Court confirmed that they were only alerted to a child witness if the indictment gave the age as part of the offence. Ages were not always given on the witness list and this posed problems in identifying young witnesses who were not victims. In the clerks' view, lack of notice meant that there was also insufficient advance planning.

Three of the sheriffs generally welcomed the receipt of child-centred information:

> 'I want to be informed about anything taking the child out of the ordinary run'

> 'I want to know about the child's attention span. We need to have lots of breaks and may only be able to sit for half a day. I also want to know something about the child's interests which will allow me to find something to talk to the child about other than the case'

> 'I would expect the fiscal to tell me of any particular learning difficulties'.

One of the Sheriffs emphasised the value of such communication in flagging questions to be avoided in building rapport with the child. Thus, if the defendant does not know where the child lives, the Sheriff should not ask which school he or she attends. Similarly, if the child is in care, questions about home life should be avoided.

However, the majority of judicial interviewees were circumspect about receiving child-centred information before the trial started:

> 'I am dubious about being given this information, although it is probably alright if it is also given to the defence'

> 'If I want information I can ask – I don't want a great flow of information all the time'

> 'We don't need to know anything about the child, unless the child is terrified – but I would want to be convinced'

> 'Some sheriffs don't want any such information'

> 'It is better not to know, though I would take a break if necessary'.

The Lord Justice General's Memorandum applies both to summary trials and those on indictment. However, some sheriffs distinguished between jury and summary trials as to how far they could modify procedures or receive information relating to child witnesses. Some took the view that certain measures were appropriate provided the jury was advised of the reasons.[76] One had developed a standard jury instruction which he delivered at the outset of child witness cases (see Annex A).

---

[76] An instruction to the jury is shown in the good practice video for judges 'A Case for Balance' NSPCC 1997

Most judges and sheriffs felt that less needed to be done to modify procedures for young witnesses who were not victims. Thus one judge said that 'there was no question of a TV link' for bystander witnesses aged 12. On the other hand, one sheriff commented that the most traumatised child witness he had dealt with was a boy of about eight who had seen his father mauled by a dog and 'relived the experience' when recounting what happened.

It was seldom possible to establish in advance of trial what arrangements would be sanctioned by the trial judge. Even if the CCTV or screen application had been approved pre-trial, it could be reviewed by the trial judge.[77] Applications for special arrangements under the Lord Justice General's Memorandum were therefore made at the start of the trial diet in the presence of the defence.[78]

Problems concerning communication of information about children which were identified during the research are summarised in the following table:

---

[77] HMA v. Birkett 1992 SCCR 850
[78] Book of Regulations 16.130

Table 3: Problems identified during Phase One concerning communication of information about young witnesses

Area of practice	Nature of problem
Inter-agency liaison	Policies emphasising consultation had not been adequately translated into practice. Rubbing points occurred where agency responsibilities were unclear. Mechanisms for obtaining and sharing information about the child were ad hoc. Children who were victims of offences outside the family fell outside any special provision. Non-evidential information about the child was not passed on systematically; those taking decisions at later stages in the process often did so with little or no information about individual children
Therapy	There was widespread confusion about whether the provision of therapy was permissible prior to the child giving evidence at court. It was believed that therapy was commonly withheld on the grounds of potential contamination
Applications for screens and CCTV	Those writing reports in support of applications assumed they would be read by the trial judge. The reports often contained information relevant to the management of the trial e.g. about the child's learning difficulties or concentration span. These reports were not routinely included in the trial judge's papers

The Lord Justice General's Memorandum:	
Consistency	The Scottish Law Commission had wanted greater 'uniformity of approach'. Judicial practice varied very widely
Content	The Memorandum advised judges to have regard to children's ages, maturity and any special factors placed before the court concerning their disposition, health or physique. However, there was no consensus about what information could be communicated
Summary trials	Some sheriffs distinguished what could be communicated to them about the child witness in summary and sheriff and jury trials, although the Memorandum applied to both
Mechanisms	There was no agreed mechanism for communicating Memorandum information to the judiciary
Timing	There was no prescribed guidance as to when information should be communicated. Child witness matters were not routinely raised at pre-trial hearings or documented in the papers for the trial sheriff
Awareness	Members of the judiciary seldom dealt with child witness cases and few had used CCTV. They had no opportunity to find out how colleagues dealt with child witness issues. They received no feedback about what had worked well or poorly. Some acknowledged that they were unaware of the Memorandum.

PHASE TWO

The Communications Pilot

The pilot subgroup was chaired by a member of the Procurator Fiscal Service and included representatives of the Strathclyde Police, Scottish Children's Reporter Administration and Glasgow Social Work Department and, in the later stages, the Scottish Courts Service and a sheriff.

The subgroup addressed the problems identified in Phase One of poor inter-agency communication of information about young witnesses by exploring ways in which the transfer of information could be made more systematic. The specific objectives were:

- to specify the nature of the information to be communicated about child witnesses, its sources, responsibilities for collecting and communicating the information, and the mechanisms for and timing of communication
- to ensure that information about the child flows through the system so that the child's needs can be addressed and decisions affecting the child's welfare can be made as early as possible
- to ensure that decision-making by the police, prosecution, reporter and judiciary can be well-informed.

Communication pilot objective: to specify the nature of the information to be communicated about child witnesses, its sources, responsibilities for collecting and communicating the information, and the mechanisms for and timing of communication

This objective was addressed through the production of a protocol written by the procurator fiscal representative, incorporating comments from other subgroup members. It contained guidance on the content of the police report in child witness cases and dealt with all categories of evidential information required by the procurator fiscal. Distribution was not restricted to pilot cases because of its general application to prosecutions involving young witnesses. For the purpose of the pilot, the subgroup agreed that the research would evaluate the response to that part of the protocol dealing with communication of non-evidential information about the child.

A checklist for distribution at inter-agency case discussions was produced to complement the protocol (both sides of the checklist are reproduced on the following pages). The checklist was aimed at all those working with child witnesses in criminal cases or children's hearing court proceedings. Case discussions were seen as an essential part of the joint agency strategy whose main purpose was to pool information about the investigation and propose a plan of action. The subgroup envisaged that the case discussion would also provide a vehicle for the exchange of 'all necessary information about the child' and allow other sources of information to be identified.

GLASGOW CHILD WITNESS SUPPORT PROJECT

CHECKLIST ON COMMUNICATING INFORMATION ABOUT CHILD WITNESSES

The list overleaf has been produced by the inter-agency Child Witness Support Project to assist all those working with child witnesses in criminal or children's hearing court proceedings.

Categories of information. The list is not exhaustive. It suggests types of information which you are encouraged to pass on to the police, reporter, procurator fiscal and the judiciary and which should be requested by them before key decisions are made which affect the child. Details should be updated as the case progresses. The information may be relevant to:

- the investigative interview
- planning a medical examination of the child
- the police report
- precognition
- planning the child's attendance at an identification parade
- decisions about presenting the child's evidence and planning attendance at court
- the choice of a support person to accompany the child.

When passing on information, always give the case name and appropriate agency reference number, if known.

Sources of information. These include the child, the parent/ carer or relative, investigative interviewer, teacher, social worker, health visitor, GP or other doctor. Doctors require the consent of the child (or, if the child is too young, the person with parental responsibility) in order to pass on health information obtained in the course of a medical examination. Exceptions may be made where the child requires protection or is in a life-threatening situation. In all cases the doctor will attempt to act in the best interests of the child.

Information for the judiciary. The Lord Justice General's Memorandum on the Treatment of Child Witnesses by the Courts (1990) states that `all children are different, and judges should take each child's particular circumstances into account before deciding what steps, if any, should be taken to minimise anxiety or distress'.

The Memorandum addresses the removal of wigs and gowns, positioning the child at a table in the well of the court, the use of supporter to sit alongside the child, and clearing the court. The checklist includes factors to be considered by the judge before taking measures suggested by the Memorandum as well as those which must be considered in relation to applications for evidence on commission, screens or CCTV (s. 271, Criminal Justice (Scotland) Act 1995). In solemn procedure sheriff and jury cases, the first diet can be used to alert the sheriff to special factors relating to child witnesses.

Confidentiality. Background information about a child witness which is gathered during the investigation and incorporated in the police report to the procurator fiscal and reporter is treated in confidence. Information communicated to the judiciary in support of an application either under the Lord Justice General's Memorandum or the provisions of Section 271 will be disclosed to the defence.

1. Maturity	does child seem to be more mature/ younger than average for his or her age?	
2. Personality	e.g. outgoing, confident, anxious, shy, sullen, withdrawn, low self-esteem	
3. Behaviour	underlying problems as well as behaviour arising after the alleged offence, e.g. bed-wetting, poor sleep, hyper-activity, restlessness, low flash point, aggression	
4. Abilities	-	to explain the difference between lying and telling the truth
	-	to estimate how long ago things happened
	-	to read and to recognise numbers
	-	to concentrate (how long is the child's normal attention span in class?)
5. Language development	-	first language if not English
	-	ability to communicate
	-	preferred ways to communicate (e.g. writing things down)
	-	level of understanding
	-	special vocabulary for parts of the body, if relevant
6. Health	-	physical characteristics e.g. wears glasses, hard of hearing
	-	regular medication e.g. for asthma
	-	special needs
7. Therapy	is it planned or underway?	
8. Home situation	e.g. removal from home	
9. Life events	e.g. moving house, previous court experience, exams	
10. Feelings about alleged offender	e.g. fear, affection, ambivalence, need to protect or appease	
11. Other people	and organisations with information about the child or the family	
12. The legal process	-	alternative ways for child to demonstrate intimate touching, if relevant (not on child's own body)
	-	suggestions for suitable person to support child at identification parade, interview/ precognition, court etc. (not a witness)
	-	the child's willingness to be a witness
	-	supportiveness of child's parents/ carers about going to court
	-	child's specific worries about going to court
	-	name of person(s) to provide information about the child's ability to testify in court (re screens/ CCTV application)
	-	child's special interests, likes and dislikes (for use as ice-breakers).
13. Information required by the judiciary	-	the child's age and maturity (LJG's Memo; 1995 Act)
	-	the nature of the charge(s) and the child's evidence (Memo; Act)
	-	relationship between the child and the alleged offender (Memo; Act)
	-	factors concerning the child's disposition, health or physique (Memo)
	-	the possible effect on the child if required to give evidence if no application is granted (Act)
	-	whether it is likely that the child would be better able to give evidence if the application is granted (Act)
	-	the views of the child (Act).

Communication pilot objectives: to ensure that information about the child flows through the system so that the child's needs can be addressed and decisions affecting the child's welfare can be made as early as possible, and to ensure that decision-making by the police, prosecution, reporter and judiciary can be well-informed

In order to evaluate implementation of these objectives, information-flow about the child and decision-making were tracked through various stages of case progress (precognition is dealt with in the next chapter). This was done through observations at case discussions, interviews with key personnel, examination of police reports, case conference and case discussion records, procurator fiscal files and, in the case of medical examinations, questionnaires completed by the examining physician.

The police report

None of the police reports prepared for the 11 cases in this pilot incorporated the categories of non-evidential information highlighted in the child witness checklist. (Most of these cases were drawn from FACU offices which had not been briefed about the project at its outset.) However, in the 17 cases monitored in the other pilots, six police reports contained a limited amount of information suggested by the checklist, mostly raising questions about the supportiveness of the child's carer. Notes were added at the end of witness statements, offering the reporting officer's assessment of the child. Procurators fiscal welcomed this information. If statements were disclosed, such notes were treated in confidence and it was therefore helpful if they were provided to the procurator fiscal on a separate page.

Communication with the reporter

Reporters were notified by the police about all cases in this pilot but not about children in six of the cases in other pilots. The reporters thought that the police should have sent subject sheets on at least some of these children. For example, one case only came to their attention because the procurator fiscal decided not to proceed, the child's carer complained about this decision and the fiscal wished to check what action the reporter was taking before seeing the carer. In that case the alleged abuser was in a household with two children but this had not been notified to the reporter. .

Practice in police FACUs varied as to whether they sent reporters subject sheets giving notice of the start of an enquiry involving a child. There was no formal agreement between the police and reporters on the timing and nature of referrals. Notice had been delayed in two cases where CID officers were unaware of the need to notify the reporter.

Reporter practice in response to such notice from the police also varied. While they sometimes made preliminary enquiries of the social work department, they usually waited until receiving the police report before deciding whether to commission a social work background report. This happened in the seven pilot cases in which reporters asked for reports. Social workers were given four weeks to provide reports although they sometimes took longer. This sequence of events meant that social work background reports were invariably collated after police reports.

Where police enquiries were conducted jointly with the social work department as happened in three pilot cases, police reports to the procurator fiscal had access to information from social work sources, but social work reports to the reporter inevitably provided more child-centred information, for example that a child in main-stream education had learning difficulties. However, such information was unlikely to be shared with the procurator fiscal unless the fiscal approached the social work department, usually in relation to an application for CCTV or screens.

The inter-agency case discussion

Case discussions or conferences chaired by the social work department and attended by police FACU officers and others were held in six pilot cases. Four were held before the submission of the police report to the procurator fiscal. These meetings did not prove to be good vehicles to feed information about the child into the criminal justice process. The child witness checklist was provided in advance to the social work department district manager or chair of these meetings but was distributed in only three cases, probably because of lack of awareness about the pilot. The checklist itself was not discussed. Forward planning at the meetings focused on immediate child protection issues. Discussions did not look further ahead to the child's needs in relation to a criminal process about which a decision was often still pending.

The minutes of these meetings often contained information relevant to the impact of the alleged offence on the child or the supportiveness of the family. For example, at one meeting a social worker reported that the child, who had been threatened by the accused with the death of the mother, was afraid of being taken away by the police and was resisting going to school. The child's behaviour was very disturbed. The police report to the procurator fiscal had already been submitted and although a police officer was present, this information was not passed on to the procurator fiscal.

Inter-agency meetings continue to be held after the submission of the police report where there are ongoing child protection concerns; however, the police may not attend if the investigation is over and the police report has already been submitted. For example, the police were not present at a meeting which discussed a child who was having nightmares about the alleged offence. Again, no-one present communicated this information to the procurator fiscal.

Decisions about the method by which children would give evidence

Applications for CCTV had been made on behalf of 12 of the 66 children in pilot cases. Requests from the procurator fiscal for information about the child tended to focus on those petition cases for which CCTV or screens was being considered. Supporting reports had been prepared by social workers, residential care workers, teachers and in one case by the procurator fiscal. Standard guidance was provided by the procurator fiscal on the framework of reports but some teachers and social workers felt the instructions were written in 'legal jargon' and not sufficiently helpful to people lacking in court experience. Some found it helpful if the procurator fiscal talked them through precisely what was required.

Reports did not confine themselves to comments on the way the child should give evidence but also provided insights about support of the child and management of the case at court:

> 'This child feels he should not be speaking about the incident' (report from a nursery teacher on a four year-old)

> 'His level of concentration and patience is limited... he has little concept of time. Asking him to wait five minutes is like asking him to wait for three hours... waiting time should be kept to a minimum... he requires a high level of support in stressful situations' (report on a 12 year-old in residential care)

> 'His experiences of the legal system have affected him negatively. He requires as much support as possible in making this experience safe' (report on a 13-year-old in residential care).

Unless CCTV or screens was under consideration, there was no systematic process to inform the procurator fiscal of up-to-date information about young witnesses before cases came to trial. Efforts to obtain information were less likely in summary cases. Such cases were less likely to be the subject of applications for screens or CCTV, witnesses were not precognosced by the prosecution, and it was unclear until late in the proceedings which prosecutor would take the trial. Communication was also problematic where the case was assigned to a temporary procurator fiscal, as happened in one pilot case. In a number of such situations, the CWO or the research team were able to pass on information to the prosecutor at court of which the prosecutor was unaware. In one example, the prosecutor thought that the girls waiting to give evidence 'were fine'; she was unaware that they had been feeling very scared and had been bed-wetting as the court date approached.

The booklet 'Your Child is a Witness', developed as part of the child witness project, encouraged carers to tell the procurator fiscal about the child's anxieties, views about how the child could best give evidence, the child's attention span, learning or other disabilities, medication taken by the child, the need for a support person and any special words in the child's vocabulary. Carers confirmed that they had not been asked by the police at the investigation stage to provide the types of information listed in the booklet and found the booklet helpful in encouraging them to ask questions and to volunteer information about the child.

Decisions about therapy

Six of the 26 pilot cases raised therapy issues illustrating the tensions between the child's welfare, concerns about contamination and uncertainty about role boundaries. In the first, a therapist had refused to see the child until the court case was over. In the second and third cases, therapists warned parents that they (the therapists) were unable to discuss with the child what had happened, even though one of these children was self-harming and his school reported that he 'wants to talk about the offence every day'. In the fourth case, the therapist asked the procurator fiscal for advice, who noted after this discussion that the therapist 'would not embark on full counselling yet'.

The fifth case concerned a young child with high anxiety levels and psychosomatic symptoms. Her behaviour was highly sexualised and her mother was 'at her wit's end' because she was afraid to let the girl out of her sight. The therapist notified the procurator fiscal that 'in view of the pre-trial status of this case it would not be appropriate to discuss the specific details of the allegations, however, it is important that M is given support to sort out her feelings and confusion'. The therapist asked permission to begin work focusing on the child's safety. In a note made nine months before the trial date, the procurator fiscal file note said:

> 'I explained this is not a good idea particularly with a view to explaining to the child what is not appropriate and giving her ideas about behaviour. This could well contaminate the evidence and I have asked that she not begin this type of programme. She [the therapist] understood..'.

The sixth case was not taken to court because of a lack of corroboration. However, the procurator fiscal noted on the file that the carer was advised that:

> 'It was important that B not discuss the case with anyone as it might create problems for her if and when she was called upon to give evidence'.

Communication with the judiciary

The protocol and checklist did not address the question of how information about young witnesses should be communicated to the court. The pilot subgroup focused on this issue in its later stages when a sheriff joined the group. It favoured the submission of a child witness report to the court at a preliminary hearing rather than waiting to address concerns at the diet of trial. The subgroup considered that information relevant for the sheriff or judge included:

- the child's needs in relation to the Lord Justice General's Memorandum
- factual matters, such as the child's interests and hobbies, to give some context to the competency examination
- information relating to management of the case, such as the need for breaks to accommodate the child's developmental age and concentration span
- information to assist in setting ground rules for examination and cross-examination, taking account of the child's abilities and level of understanding.

The sheriff raised with the subgroup the continuing problem of reports supporting CCTV applications not remaining with court papers when the case came to trial. This was drawn to the attention of the Sheriff Principal in Glasgow so that steps could be taken to ensure that reports were married up with the case papers at trial. The Scottish Court Service advised that although there was no written policy on this point, it was practice for the papers to be kept with the complaint or indictment and to be available to the trial judge or sheriff.

Only one case in this pilot went to trial during the fieldwork period but it provided a valuable example of what could be achieved by pre-trial communication and advance planning. The procurator fiscal asked the sheriff presiding at the first diet to take a note for the trial sheriff about the needs of the child witnesses, aged four and five. The sheriff did not do so but identified the trial sheriff. The procurator fiscal and defence lawyer asked jointly to see the trial sheriff in chambers the week before the trial. This meeting was used to plan the staggered attendance of the children at court, the use of a support person in the CCTV room and the testing of competency in the jury's presence. It was also agreed that the sheriff and lawyers would introduce themselves to the children in the CCTV room before they gave their evidence and that wigs and gowns would be removed. The sheriff felt that the planning meeting was a useful model for the management of cases in future. The trial was described as proceeding smoothly, with minimum distress to the young children, by all involved including the parent and support person. The case resulted in a conviction.

One of the non-pilot cases observed at trial illustrated the problems of lack of advance planning. The principal witness was a seven-year-old with cerebral palsy. No arrangement had been made for the family to use parking for the disabled at court even though the child was in a wheelchair. The child had arrived at court at 9.45 am but was not called until the afternoon. Her mother asked the procurator fiscal whether there was a possibility that a screen could be used but did not get a response. Before the trial started, the sheriff was asked to take off his wig but agreed to clear the court. During the child's evidence, her mother offered her a drink of water and was admonished by the sheriff. The girl was asked to make a dock identification but did not have her glasses. After a debate, it was decided that she could be wheeled round the court and she then made the identification. During cross-examination, she broke down in tears without intervention by the sheriff or procurator fiscal. The mother also began crying. A partial plea had been offered in this case but was not accepted. The jury returned a not proven verdict. The mother shouted that she should never have allowed her daughter to come to court.

Communication concerning medical examinations

Forensic medical examination of a child witness was not a basis for referral to the pilot project but it was agreed that where examinations occurred in any pilot case, specific questions could be addressed to the doctor. Information was requested concerning medical examinations of ten children in eight cases of alleged sexual assault.

Children in three cases were seen by a consultant paediatrician (in two cases, jointly with another hospital physician) and in five cases by a police casualty surgeon. Children seen at hospital had either been brought to the accident and emergency room by family members or referred by the social work department, whereas police surgeon cases had been referred for examination by the police or the procurator fiscal. Reports were provided in all cases to the police or procurator fiscal. In all three hospital cases and one examination conducted by a police surgeon, information was also provided to the social work department or GP. Only children in the hospital cases had medical follow-up or were referred for therapy. A hospital report in one case included the observation that the mother had not touched or sat near to the child and that the aunt was 'clearly more supportive' (information relevant to considerations about who should support the child at court). In another case, the hospital report conveyed information to the procurator fiscal about the child's behaviour and how her anxiety manifested itself.

According to policy, the sole purpose of the examination should not be to gather evidence.[79] It is good practice to conduct a full medical examination into the general health of the child and obtain the consent of both the guardian and child, where the child is of sufficient maturity.[80] The paediatricians and two of the five police surgeons reported taking the child's previous medical history. All reported addressing the question of consent.

Police policy stated that medical examinations should not be done automatically because of the potentially traumatic effect on the child and the possibility that no conclusive evidence will be found.[81] In their questionnaire responses, all doctors said that they had been given information about the time interval since the last alleged offence and all but two (both police surgeons) had discussed with the person accompanying the child whether a medical examination for evidential purposes was appropriate.

In the hospital cases, a relative supported the child at the examination; at the police office, a police officer was present. Doctors were asked about the explanations given to children to prepare them for the examination. The paediatricians apparently went into greater detail about this than the police surgeons, for example 'the roles of the personnel involved, a tour of the unit, the equipment used and the child's ability to control what happened and to say 'stop' at any time'. In another hospital case, the child had a preliminary visit to the unit one day and the medical examination the following day.

---

[79] Book of Regulations 16.55
[80] Book of Regulations 16.57; Strathclyde Police (June 1993)
[81] Strathclyde Police (June 1993)

IDENTIFICATION OF THE ACCUSED

PHASE ONE FINDINGS

The study examined policy and practice associated with children's attendance at identification parades and the requirement of in-court identification of the accused (otherwise known as 'dock identification') which is a hallmark of Scottish legal procedure:

> 'Even where a previous identification parade has taken place, it is customary in Scotland for a witness to be asked to identify in court the person whom he or she has been talking about in evidence. Likewise, an in-court identification will frequently be sought even where the witness is talking about a friend or relative, and where there is really no dispute that the accused is the friend or relative being referred to'.[82]

Interviewees reported that dock identifications by child witnesses were common. Sheriffs agreed that 'the child will almost certainly have to identify the accused at court'. One observed:

> 'It is a great booster to credibility if the child is upset at the sight of the accused. This is a strong motivation for the fiscal to leave identification to the courtroom'.

Confronting the accused is one of the greatest sources of anxiety for child witnesses. Pointing out the accused in court[83] or at an identification parade can be extremely stressful. Research has confirmed that some children are distressed even when participating in a simulated identification parade: 'The majority... were nervous, embarrassed and even frightened. Children had to be coaxed... and even then they were unwilling to look at the men'.[84] In another experiment, children who failed to identify the 'thief' at the parade told their parents later that they had recognised him but were afraid to identify him 'in case something bad might happen'.[85] In both of these studies, a higher proportion of children made correct identifications from photographs than at the parade.

During Phase One, police interviewees reported that children were seldom asked to observe parades except in cases of stranger assault. Where parades were held, Crown Office policy encouraged the use of a one-way screen, a demonstration of its use and procedures tailoring the conduct of the parade to suit the child, for example by using symbols for a child unable to

---

[82] Report on the Evidence of Children and Other Vulnerable Witnesses (1990) Scottish Law Commission para. 3.7

[83] K. Murray (1995) Preparing Child Witnesses for Court para. 8.45

[84] H. Dent and G. Stephenson (1979) Identification evidence: experimental investigations of factors affecting the reliability of juvenile and adult witnesses. In D. Farrington et al (eds.) Psychology, Law and Legal Processes. Atlantic Highlands NJ: Humanities Press

[85] D. Peters (1991) The influence of stress and arousal on the child witness. In J. Doris (ed.) The Suggestibility of Children's Recollections. Washington: American Psychological Association

recognise numbers.[86] However, formal police instructions on the conduct of parades laid down by the Lord Advocate did not explain how procedures could be modified to accommodate a child's needs. For example, police officers frequently simplified the wording of the standard parade form to take account of the child's level of understanding but these changes were made on an ad hoc basis and the precise words used were not always noted in the police report of the parade. There was no guidance about the role of a supporter for the child at the parade or who might be appropriate to carry out this function.

Where identification evidence existed or could be established other than by dock identification at trial, procurators fiscal were expected to consider carefully whether it was necessary to have the child identify the accused in court. Alternative methods included:

- an identification parade
- selection from a sample of photographs
- reference to a photograph, for example where the accused is a relative
- the child pointing out the accused to a third party prior to the trial[87]
- naming the accused, where this is a relative.[88]

Police and procurators fiscal acknowledged that these alternative methods to a dock identification were seldom used and were not considered consistently or at a sufficiently early stage. For example, a third party who could confirm the child's identification of the accused needed to be named for this purpose in the indictment.

The Lord Advocate required the police to inform the procurator fiscal about children falling within the statutory criteria for eligibility for CCTV, screens and evidence on commission and to 'detail the available evidence' relating to identification because 'use of one of the statutory methods may be dependent on there being sufficient admissible evidence of a prior identification by the child'.[89] The Lord Advocate's guidance described early identification of eligible cases as 'essential'. If an application was contemplated and the child had not previously identified the accused to a third party, prosecutors were expected to instruct the police to hold an identification parade.[90] The Crown Office recommended that if identification was not in dispute, a joint minute should be sought from the defence 'as a matter of course'.[91] However even in cases of offences within the family, procurators fiscal often did not know until the trial whether identification would be raised as an issue by the defence, making a dock identification necessary.

---

[86] The officer in charge of the parade had responsibility to record any special arrangements and ensure that variations from the standard procedure were fair: Book of Regulations 16.63

[87] Book of Regulations 16.120; section 271(11), Criminal Procedure (Scotland) Act 1995. This provision is in addition to the position at common law and to the hearsay provisions of section 260

[88] Book of Regulations 16.136. In such circumstances the prosecutor had to lead evidence to link prior identification to an identification of the accused in court: Crown Office note for Working Group meeting (20 March 1996)

[89] Guidelines issued by the Lord Advocate to Chief Constables on the provisions relating to children's evidence in section 271 of the Criminal Procedure (Scotland) Act 1995

[90] Book of Regulations 16.62

[91] Book of Regulations 16.132

Uncertainty about how the child's evidence would be presented and the possible need for a dock identification was described as very problematic for young witnesses by those supporting them. It also curtailed attempts to address their anxieties, as prosecutors were unable to respond to children's questions about where the accused would be in court.

PHASE TWO

The Identification Pilot

The identification pilot subgroup was chaired by a Strathclyde Police representative; other members represented the Procurator Fiscal Service, Crown Office, Scottish Children's Reporter Administration and the Law Society of Scotland. Given its membership, the subgroup described itself as 'a natural focus for co-ordinating the broad range of activities directed at improving the welfare and lessening the anxiety of child witnesses'. The subgroup drew up an action plan which addressed the use of identification parades and dock identification by the child at court. Its objectives, as revised during the course of the project, were as follows:

- to introduce early contact between the police and the procurator fiscal to ensure that evidential issues in relation to identification are resolved, having regard *inter alia* to the means by which the child may ultimately give evidence at court
- to formalise good practice into a protocol for officers conducting parades and guidance on briefing child witnesses prior to the parade.

The Working Group wished to explore greater use of alternative methods of identification evidence and reduce where possible the need for child witnesses to make a dock identification. Initial discussions were informed by a study of closed cases which had presented problems of identification evidence, including one in which the question of dock identification was raised with children at court who had previously been assured that they would not see the accused. The social worker in that case queried why the matter had not been discussed earlier: 'How identification evidence should be addressed should be as much of a consultation process as the medical examination'.

The first version of the subgroup's pilot objectives referred to greater use of options, as set out in Crown Office policy, to lessen dock identifications. Thus in one of the other pilot protocols the procurator fiscal stated that 'The ideal is to avoid the confrontational dock identification and to rely on such things as an identification parade or some other method of identification involving members of the family or others'.

However, when the first identification pilot case reached court, the objective of lessening the need for dock identifications had to be reconsidered. This case involved children who made a positive identification of the accused (a stranger) in an identification parade and were also asked to make a dock identification at the trial. In subsequent group discussions, it was decided that the pilot case had correctly followed the case law in Robson v HMA 1996 SCCR 340 which had narrowed the options available to the procurator fiscal regarding the presentation of identification evidence. In Robson, two young witnesses gave evidence but were not asked to identify the accused in court. Instead, circumstantial detail as to identification was provided by the children's parents. Although this was rejected as a ground of appeal, the court observed that 'it was difficult to understand why the Crown did not comply with the general rule requiring that identification be the subject of an express question and that the accused must be directly identified by being pointed to or described by the witness by reference to his position in court...'.

In August 1997, the Crown Office Standing Committee on Children considered the implications of Robson and decided that procurators fiscal should follow the ruling laid down in the case of Bruce v HMA 1936 JC 93, seeking a dock identification in all cases where children give evidence by conventional means. Advice from the procurator fiscal to the police emphasised that "humanitarian reasons' do not justify a departure from this rule. It is only once it has been established that the child is unable or unwilling to identify the accused that reliance may be placed on other evidence of identification'.[92] The objectives of the identification pilot were therefore revised to omit consideration of alternatives to dock identification.

The pilot objectives had also originally included consideration of the need or otherwise for an identification parade. During the course of the pilot, however, procurators fiscal recommended that parades be conducted automatically during the seven day remand period or as a condition of bail whenever an application for CCTV or screens was a possibility. A parade was necessary to leave open decisions about how the child would give evidence which would not be taken until near the trial'.[93] Applications for screens or CCTV would 'therefore not be sought if identification cannot be established in advance'. Conducting a parade was good practice even where 'the child complainer and the accused were related or otherwise well-known to one another'.[94]

In light of these restrictions on the range of options available for the presentation of identification evidence, the pilot objectives were amended to omit consideration of the need or otherwise for an identification parade.

Identification pilot objective: to introduce early contact between the police and the procurator fiscal to ensure that evidential issues in relation to identification are resolved, having regard inter alia to the means by which the child may ultimately give evidence at court

The subgroup had intended that the seven cases selected for this pilot would involve allegations in which the accused was a family member or was known to the child. Due to the shortage of referrals, a wider range of cases was accepted. In four pilot cases, the accused was not a member of the family or otherwise well known to the child. The police held parades on their own initiative in two of these cases and parades were instructed by the

---

[92] Letter from assistant procurator fiscal to police officer who chaired the identification subgroup, 2 September 1997
[93] Op. cit.
[94] Internal Procurator Fiscal's Office memorandum, 1 October 1997

procurator fiscal in the other two. The three remaining pilot cases involved members of the family or people familiar to the household. The procurator fiscal directed that a parade be held in two cases and the police held a parade without consultation in the third.

It was considered good practice for the police to ask the accused to confirm in interview that he knew the child witness. This was done in five pilot cases. However, defence lawyers acknowledged that even where there was a close relationship between the accused and the child witness, the question of identification evidence was unlikely to be formally conceded at an early stage. A joint minute concerning identification was agreed in one pilot case, but only on the morning of trial just before the entry of a guilty plea.

Procurators fiscal and police officers were in agreement that parades were appropriate in cases in which the accused was not a member of the family or otherwise well known to the child. However, many FACU officers expressed disquiet about extending the requirement of parades to family members. Parades were directed in two cases in other pilots in which the accused persons were the victims' father and brother. In the latter case, the reporting officer said:

> 'I was having difficulty finding stand-ins and then I thought to myself "This is ridiculous, why should it matter what they look like? She is always going to be able to pick out her brother." On the day, the defence didn't object that the line-up did not look anything like the accused'.

Table 4: Relationship to the accused and identification parades

Relationship of the accused to first child	Was there an identification parade? (all pilot cases)		
	no	yes	Total
household/other relative	11	4	15
known adult	2	3	5
stranger	1	5	6
Total	14	12	26

There was a tension between avoiding the child's attendance at a parade before it was decided by the procurator fiscal that the case would proceed to court and asking a child to attend a parade many months after the investigative interview. In five cases, the accused was charged within days of the offence being reported and in four of these a parade was held not long afterwards. (In the fifth, no parade was held because the child witnesses' parents would not let them attend.) In the two remaining cases which began by way of petition, the procurator fiscal asked for participation in the parade as a condition of bail. These parades took place three months and seven months respectively after the children had been interviewed.

Some police officers believed that it was not in the child's interests to 'endure the potential trauma of a parade' prior to the procurator fiscal's decision whether to proceed with the case or a decision to apply for CCTV or screens.[95] FACU officers said that parades were held in order to keep the statutory options open for a later decision by the procurator fiscal, not as a result of detailed consideration of how the child might give evidence at court. Carers confirmed that the question of how the child might give evidence had not been discussed with them at the stage at which decisions were made about holding the parade.

Police officers were also concerned about the resource implications of an increased number of parades. In November 1997, one FACU calculated that in the previous 12 months it had dealt with 30 cases in which there was sufficient evidence to substantiate charges. Parades had been conducted at the direction of the procurator fiscal in three cases of stranger assault. In the remainder, the accused and the child complainer were known to one another. As a result of the policy changes at the start of the pilot, the unit foresaw a possible 90 per cent increase in the number of parades required and argued that each case should be dealt with on its own circumstances, bearing in mind other forms of identification and the accused's admissions.

Following further subgroup discussions, in May 1998 the subgroup's procurator fiscal representative drafted a note to assist investigating officers, distinguishing when a parade was required and when it was merely desirable:[96]

---

[95] Identification parades November 1996-November 1997: Overview prepared for November 1997 meeting between the police and procurators fiscal
[96] Child Witness Support Project: Note re Identification Parades. Procurator Fiscal's Office (1998)

> **Procurator Fiscal Note re Identification Parades**
>
> This note is designed to assist investigating officers to decide whether an identification parade should be held.
>
> **A parade may be required in the following circumstances**
>
> - where it is necessary for evidential reasons i.e. where a parade is required in order to establish whether there is sufficient evidence to identify a suspect as the perpetrator of a crime
> - where it is desirable for evidential reasons e.g. where witness identification is likely to weaken if there is a delay before the case comes to trial
>
> (The above circumstances may arise where the suspect is not already known to the witness)
>
> - where there is a likelihood that a child or vulnerable witness may give evidence using CCTV or a screen or on commission.
>
> Where evidence is given by such methods the witness will not be permitted to make an identification in open court. Thus if identification evidence from that witness is required it will be necessary to lead evidence of his/ her earlier identification of the accused. If such identification cannot be established by other means a parade will be required.

The note went on to explain that in relation to CCTV, screens or evidence on commission there was no statutory requirement that evidence of a previous identification must relate to identification at a formal parade. If the child had identified the accused by some other means (e.g. by pointing out the accused to another witness) 'such evidence may be adequate'.

The note concluded that where a child gave evidence in open court, 'in most cases he will be invited to identify in court <u>even if evidence of a prior identification</u> (such as identification at a parade) is available' (emphasis in original).

Identification pilot objective: to formalise good practice into a protocol for officers conducting parades and guidance on briefing child witnesses prior to the parade

Parades were held in six of the seven pilot cases: in the seventh, a parade was instructed but the parent of the young witnesses refused to let them attend. Five parades were observed by the researchers in this pilot as well as two in other pilot cases. Young witnesses identified the accused in all these cases. Towards the end of the pilot, the researchers provided feedback to the subgroup from these observations and discussions with young witnesses and their escorts, police officers and defence representatives. The findings were used by the subgroup to draft four guidance documents, not only for the child witness and officer conducting the parade as originally planned, but also for the officer in charge of the investigation and for the person accompanying the child.

Carers in five of the six pilot cases in which parades were held said they and their children had wanted more information beforehand. One anxious child was briefed by his teacher's spouse who was a police officer. A few families were visited by the reporting officer ahead of time but most were notified about the parade by telephone, often with only 24 hours notice. Young children in only one case were given a preparatory visit to the parade suite on the day before the parade.

While waiting at the police station, children and their supporters were given explanations before viewing the parade. In all but one case, the formal wording was paraphrased when read to the children in the waiting room, the amended language having been agreed with the defence. The children were usually asked if they had any questions. It was helpful for them to receive instructions before going into the parade room but even so, anxiety on the day sometimes limited their ability to take in information. Children said, for example:

> 'It was all a bit too nerve wracking to think of questions – it all happened in a blur'

> 'I didn't hear the words of the police officer in the room. We couldn't possibly concentrate'.

Few children asked questions after being briefed; when they did, nearly all focused on whether the accused would be able to see them. One eight year-old waited until the police officers had left the waiting room to ask his mother what 'resemble' meant. Mothers of children who had attended in a group said that it would be preferable if the children could be asked individually if they had any questions because they were too embarrassed to speak up.

Several carers described the atmosphere at the police station on the day of the parade as inhibiting:

> 'It felt silly to ask questions when the police were so tense'

> 'The police are all tense and that makes the rest of us tense and nervous'

> 'The police were very rigid – it should all have been slowed down'.

The formality affected the children too. One ten-year-old said:

> 'If the police woman had sat down and explained it like a friend it would have been much better'.

Such feedback was used at the end of the project by the pilot subgroup in drafting the information booklet for young witnesses which explained about what a witness does; the meaning of 'breaking the law'; the purpose of the identification parade; how the one way screen works; and how a young witness can help. Additional information was provided for teenagers. The booklet for the child's supporter gave advice on preparation for the parade; the constraints on their role; and what happens after the parade. The subgroup envisaged that where possible, these booklets would be given out before the day of the parade.

Feedback from pilot cases underlined the need to ensure that the detective responsible for the conduct of the parade (an officer independent of the investigation) was appropriately briefed about the needs and abilities of the child witness by the reporting officer in charge of the investigation. Although the reporting officer generally ensured that children were sufficiently numerate to be able to pick out a member of the line-up by number, carers said they seldom asked more generally about their children's abilities or state of mind about participation.

The pilot subgroup's checklist for the reporting officer emphasised advance planning because this person plays no part in the parade and was not routinely present at the police station when children attended (this needed to be explained to children and their carers who were sometimes confused by the absence of 'their' officer). The checklist described the information about the child that needed to be obtained and passed on. While the officer conducting the parade in one pilot case was notified about a young witness with learning difficulties, the police were unaware that one child attending a parade in another case was on medication for attention deficit disorder and another had a hearing problem. At least two children attended parades without their glasses. The reporting officer's checklist also provided guidance on the explanations and demonstrations of the one-way screen that children should receive before viewing the parade.

The checklist for the officer running the identification parade advised on tailoring language and procedure to the needs and abilities of the child while remaining fair to the accused, discussing modifications to standard procedure with the defence, documenting such changes and conducting 'exit' statements after the parade. The guidance stressed the need to assure witnesses that they would not confront the accused when leaving the police station. It was important to explore these practical arrangements with the children's carers. At one parade, the children's father asked the police several times whether it would be possible for the family to leave before the accused. He was told this was not possible but there was no explanation (i.e. that an accused on bail cannot be detained beyond the conduct of the parade itself) or enquiry about why he was concerned. Later, the father reported that the children had just arrived at their grandmother's home where they were to meet their mother when the accused arrived in a taxi. Their mother refused to send them out again and the father had to call the police.

The checklists for both police roles emphasised the need to pass on information about children who did not cope well with the parade (highly relevant to any decision relating to screens or CCTV) or if the supporter did not appear to be an appropriate choice to accompany the child at court. For example, one supporter was tearful at the parade and acknowledged afterwards that she was recalling her own distress when participating in a parade.

It was important to check with the child and supporter how the child had dealt with the parade, both in the parade room and afterwards. While some children coped well at the parade, the majority described themselves or were described by their supporters as frightened of seeing the accused. Some officers involved with the parade underestimated the impact on the child: a seven-year-old assessed by officers as 'not distressed or anxious' was described by her mother as 'upset and shaking badly' after viewing the parade.

Of the seventeen young witnesses aged between six and 16 who were observed taking part in parades, one nine year-old was sufficiently comfortable to ask the officer in charge of the parade to have the men on the line-up speak and turn around. After he made the identification, the boy said 'I made it difficult for him'. None of the others felt so confident. Six began to be tearful in the parade room or immediately after leaving it and two of these, a boy of six and a girl of 14, became very distressed. When the six-year-old came into the parade room, he went up close to the window and froze as soon as he saw the accused. His fists were clenched up into his jacket and he did not speak. The officer in charge of the parade tried to break the tension by asking him to walk along the window and look at all the faces but the boy was rooted to the spot. After a long silence, the child said the number and the accused's name, then ran to his supporter. An escorting officer described this boy as 'freaking out' after leaving the parade room.

Carers complained about waiting time (up to an hour in some cases before the parade began), the cramped waiting room and the lack of magazines or comics. However, the most serious and frequently expressed concern was the physical environment of the parade. The room in which the witness stands measured approximately five feet from the back wall to the one way screen; the back wall of the room in which the line-up takes place is about 11 feet further away. When the parade is taking place, the witness room is in darkness except for a small light on a podium for the papers of the officer in charge of the parade. In contrast, the parade room seen through the one way glass is brightly light.

The lighting in the witness room was not always dimmed during visits in which the one way mirror was demonstrated, and children commented on being able to see shadows through the glass. At the parade itself, children and carers were sometimes taken aback by the darkness and how close they were to the line-up when entering the witness room. Even after the demonstration, some were sure the accused could see them:

> 'He was too close. He was looking right at me'

> 'The people in the line-up were way too close. It was horrible. If there was some distance it might have made it easier. It was as if he could reach out his hand and touch us'

> 'It was very dark on our side and very bright where the men were – it's like they were magnified'

> 'The men all seemed too close to us – it was all too small, tight spaces'

'There shouldn't be a door between our room and theirs' (there was no handle on the door on the parade room side but few of the children were told this)

'The room looked different with the lights out on our side. It really seemed as if the line-up could see in'.

The feeling of oppression was increased for some by the number of doors and small spaces passed through on the way to the parade room. One carer said 'It was like Fort Knox with all those doors'.

For those children who realised that the people on the line-up could hear anyone who spoke in the witness room, fear that the accused recognised their voice was another source of anxiety. After coming out of the parade suite, one child asked repeatedly whether her father had heard her. Another girl asked if she could hold her fingers to indicate the suspect's parade number rather than saying it aloud. The officer in charge of the parade said that it was fortunate that the defence agent agreed, otherwise this could not have been done. Such officers were reluctant to depart from standard procedure on behalf of a child witness in the absence of official guidance:

'In every case I use the standard language verbatim. I don't see the point of changing the words and running the risk of being questioned by the defence in court'.

To encourage a more sensitive response, the checklist emphasised that 'Officers conducting ID parades should be prepared to justify in court special provisions or deviations from the standard procedure but should not hesitate in doing so, if required'.

Dock identification

One objective of the research was to examine the circumstances in which children were asked to make a dock identification and its impact. By the end of the fieldwork out of all the pilot cases, seven children had given evidence in open court. Three had previously identified the accused at a parade and did so again in court. Two had not been asked to attend a parade but made a dock identification. The two remaining children failed to speak to the incident in question or to make a dock identification.

One of these children was the complainer in a trial in which the Crown had to offer no further evidence. In that case, the boy had been knocked out by a brick allegedly thrown by the accused in a fight among a group of youths. The victim had failed to attend an identification parade. At the beginning of his testimony, this 12-year-old complainer was asked to give his address, and when he did so quietly he was asked to speak up. He failed to speak to the original complaint.

The other child who was unable to make a dock identification was a witness in a summary trial which was able to proceed on the basis of the evidence of other young witnesses. The procurator fiscal who conducted the trial said that as the children had taken part in the parade, he did not think they were likely to have a problem with a dock identification at court. He described dock identification as 'the icing on the cake' and would always ask for it unless he had knowledge that it would cause a particular problem for the child. In this case, he had no such information. Interviews were conducted a month after the trial with the parents of two seven year-old witnesses who had made a dock identification in this trial. They considered this had had an adverse impact on their children, both of whom had been traumatised since the incident. One reported that her child had been waking up at night screaming that the accused was 'coming to get her' and saying over and over that she did not want to see him:

> 'I don't know why she had to do this [the dock ID]. The fiscal had already questioned her about picking him out at the parade and she answered it all. I believe she would be much better now if she hadn't had to face him again'.

The mother of the other seven-year-old reported that her child had been bedwetting and having bad dreams. The girl was very anxious and afraid to go out. Her mother described the girl as 'doing alright' in court but immediately feeling 'rotten' afterwards. The mother also complained about the dock identification:

> 'Why did she have to do that again? It's ridiculous from the child's point of view. I shouldn't have let her go to court, she might have forgotten all about it by now'.

Some children felt under pressure when asked to make a dock identification, both from the accused and the prosecution: one ten year-old said that she had not wanted to look at the accused in court. She was scared and looked everywhere else for a while; if he looked at her 'then you were a part of him, he knew your name'. One 12 year-old said of the dock identification: 'Well you would say it was him because you would be scared they would be angry with you by then'. Another 12 year-old said: 'I wish you didn't have to see the person. It's not just about being safe, it's about memories too'.

The situation was further complicated because throughout most of the pilot, parents were being told by the police that participating in a parade meant that children would not have to identify the accused at court. This was reinforced by routine correspondence from the procurator fiscal to the police instructing that a parade be held and giving the same explanation:

> 'Having a parade will avoid C having to identify the accused in court should the matter go to trial'.

All but one of the eight sheriffs interviewed in Phase Two of the study thought that it was not essential to have both an identification parade and a dock identification where the child witness knew the accused.[97] They were generally willing to accept identification proved by other means and thought that identification evidence should be sorted out at a preliminary diet. One said:

---

[97] The sheriffs did not discuss the interpretations of case law on this point

'Have a parade where identification is a real issue and the case stands or falls on this. Identification could usually be done by another route and would not need a dock ID. I wouldn't expect it. Identification is an area where unnecessary stress can be placed on the child if it is not an issue. Why put them through it?'.

INTERVIEWS AND PRECOGNITIONS

PHASE ONE FINDINGS

Multiple interviews about the alleged offence are a significant source of stress for young witnesses: 'Each successive interview necessitates a retelling of experiences that are embarrassing, frightening and anxiety-provoking.'[98] 'If the victim and family need to prepare for and endure interviews less often, then preoccupation with the offence and its outcome will be decreased'.[99] The greater the number of pre-trial interviewers, the more likely that the process will be rated as harmful.[100] Research which concluded that the number of interviews increased the level of trauma, recommended multi-disciplinary teams and greater inter-agency cooperation.[101]

Multiple interviews may also affect the quality of the child's testimony. A review of many research studies which examined the effect of repeated interviews on accuracy concluded that 'the use of multiple interviews with specific questions could not be recommended, especially for children who would be testifying after relatively long delays' because the information elicited by such interviews was more likely to be inaccurate.[102] Describing a case in which she was the eleventh person to speak to a three-year-old child, a child psychologist emphasised the risks inherent in repeated questioning:

> 'If children are interviewed many times, they lose those characteristics which help me, or later on help a sheriff, to judge their credibility. Those characteristics are spontaneity and emotional immediacy. They begin to try to protect themselves from the questioning, their accompanying emotional reactions become masked, their communications become contaminated by previous interviewers. Ultimately, and particularly in a court setting, they may resort to retraction in an attempt to protect themselves. They are then seen as having lied in the first place. We should <u>expect</u> retractions if we treat children in this way' (emphasis in original).[103]

Although no baseline data was were available, reports of multiple interviews were common. Scottish parents have reported that their children 'found the frequent interviews (as many as

---

[98] J. Yuille et al. (1993) The Effects of Children Reviewing their Initial Videotaped Interviews on Subsequent Recall for an Interactive Event. Paper for the Ministry of the Attorney General of British Columbia, Canada

[99] B. Bernstein and L. Claman (1986) Modern Technology and the Child Witness. Child Welfare, 65, pp. 155-163

[100] J. Tedesco and S. Schnell (1987) Children's reactions to sex abuse. Investigation and litigation. Child Abuse and Neglect, Vol. 11 pp. 267-72

[101] J. Henry (1997) System Intervention Trauma to Child Sexual Abuse Victims Following Disclosure, 12 Journal of Interpersonal Violence 499

[102] D. Poole and L. White (1995) Tell me Again and Again: Stability and change on the repeated testimonies of children and adults. In M. Zaragoza et al. (eds) Memory and Testimony in the Child Witness. Sage Publications p.30

[103] J. Mackinnon (1989) The Psychological Examination of the Child. In F. Stone (ed) Child Abuse: the Scottish Experience. British Agencies for Adoption and Fostering Discussion Series 11

30 in one case) very distressing and likened it to re-living the abuse many times over'.[104] Child witnesses could be questioned about the alleged offence by the police, social workers, the doctor conducting a medical examination, the procurator fiscal or precognition officer, the reporter, curator and safeguarder as well as by agents for the accused and separately represented parties to children's hearing court proceedings.

Despite the possibility of multiple interviews and their potential to affect the child's account, there was no provision for young witnesses to review their initial statement to refresh their memory before giving evidence in criminal or children's hearing court proceedings.[105] A procurator fiscal suggested that one way forward would be for the police officer and social worker to encourage the child to write down what had happened. This note could become a production which could then be shown to the child.

Lord Clyde's Report of the Inquiry into the Removal of Children from Orkney in February 1991 (1992) envisaged a co-ordinated approach that would limit the number of times young witnesses were interviewed. Police and procurator fiscal policy documents were in agreement about the need to avoid repetitive interviews and the problems which they cause to children.[106] The police acknowledged that ideally, children should be interviewed only once.[107] Effective interviewing, combined with close liaison between professional agencies:

> 'could reduce the number of times which they are called upon to repeat their accounts during the investigation of the case and thereby reduce the psychological impact that continuing recollection can cause'.[108]

Child witnesses were precognosced by a procurator fiscal or precognition officer in petition cases (precognition is not routine in summary proceedings). Prosecutors acknowledged that routine precognition did not 'sit well' with concerns about re-interviewing and they were aware of the adverse effects of multiple interviews and significant delays before trial on the child's recollection. However, they did not feel able to rely solely on the police interview given their responsibility to conduct an independent evaluation:

> 'Precognition is about testing the evidence, hopefully subtly. We always get fresh and relevant information, otherwise we wouldn't do it'.

---

[104] K. Murray (1997) Preparing Child Witnesses for Court. Scottish Office Central Research Unit

[105] In England and Wales, witnesses are entitled to see their statement to refresh their recollection before giving evidence. Videotaped interviews used for this purpose are not considered to contaminate the child's evidence but may, in some situations, facilitate the child's ability to communicate: Yuille et al. (1993) The Effects of Children Reviewing their Initial Videotaped Interviews on Subsequent Recall for an Interactive Event. Paper for the Ministry of the Attorney General of British Columbia, Canada

[106] For example, Book of Regulations 16.46; Strathclyde Police (June 1993); 'When Children Speak...' Report of a Working Group set up by the Secretary of State for Scotland and the Lord Advocate (1995)

[107] Strathclyde Police (4 May 1995)

[108] Strathclyde Police (June 1993); see also Report of a Working Group set up by the Secretary of State for Scotland and the Lord Advocate (June 1995)

Some procurators fiscal felt that the way forward was to improve the quality of police interviews. Others noted the limitations of a paper record and the difficulty for the police of getting the nuances and the child's body language on paper, something overcome in jurisdictions which videotape the investigative interview with the child.

An accused person in Scotland has no right to see police statements or Crown precognitions which are private communications made in the course of a criminal investigation on behalf of the Crown. Instead, the defence representative can precognosce all prosecution witnesses. Procurators fiscal can show police statements and Crown precognitions to the defence with a view to encouraging appropriate pleas and rendering defence precognition of the child unnecessary.[109] Procurators fiscal indicated that this discretion was exercised selectively and depended on the identity of the defence agent. Preliminary discussion between procurators fiscal and the defence may make it possible to restrict the matters discussed with the child to the contentious aspects of the evidence.[110] However, none of the interviewees engaged in preliminary discussions for this purpose.

Reporters wanted to see children before children's hearing court proceedings for the purpose of assessment and information-giving. They had no written policy on whether to precognosce although this was not encouraged in training; it was recognised that precognition could be inappropriate because of the quality of the police interview or the need to avoid upsetting the child.[111] Practice varied from those reporters who never precognosced children to those who did it routinely. Curators and safeguarders also said that they usually discussed the evidence with the child. Reporters pointed out that, unlike criminal proceedings, the defence did not have a right to precognosce the reporter's witnesses for children's hearings court proceedings, even in offence cases, but felt that attempts to prevent it would result in a complaint. When notification of the proof diet was served, it was good practice for reporters to offer copies of the child's police statement or precognition to the legal representative of the family (or of the child in an offence case).[112] In practice, reporters varied on how far to go to discourage defence precognition. Some felt under no obligation even to give the defence sight of the reporter's precognition.

Procurators fiscal and reporters did not always know whether defence agents had precognosced the child. No-one was responsible for co-ordinating the process on the child's behalf. They were therefore unable to confirm to what extent giving sight of the precognition or police statement was successful in forestalling the defence from conducting its own precognition.

There was no mechanism to alert reporters and procurators fiscal of one another's intention to interview the child. Procurators fiscal said that, even where the prosecution was still pending,

---

[109] Book of Regulations 16.84-85, 16.97
[110] Book of Regulations 16.86
[111] Reporter to the Children's Panel, Strathclyde (2 March 1995)
[112] Reporter to the Children's Panel, Strathclyde (2 March 1995)

they often gave reporters sight of precognitions and police statements.[113] Reporters, however, did not feel confident that they were always able to obtain information relevant to child protection issues and some were reluctant to ask. They described their access to Crown precognitions as 'not routine' and considered that the welfare of the child was not paramount when questions of disclosure from the prosecution arose:

> 'Crown Office policy gives priority to the criminal process; proofs do not even have parity'.

Interviewees raised other concerns about the conduct of precognitions. These included:

- carers feeling pressured to comply with precognition requests and having nowhere to register complaints about the way they were conducted
- the use of precognoscers not trained in interviewing children
- unannounced visits at the child's home by defence precognition agents
- requests to interview the child without anyone else present
- multiple precognitions where there were several accused in a criminal case or parallel proof, custody or access proceedings.

During Phase One, 11 defence solicitors were asked whether the potential number of child witness interviews could be reduced without prejudicing the rights of the accused in criminal proceedings or parties at proof hearings. Five felt that this was not possible as the interests of the parties were 'fundamentally different'. However, six thought that there was scope for the number of interviews to be reduced through greater co-ordination and increased provisions for disclosure. Their suggestions included:

- controlling the number of interviews with children
- having the original interviewer go back to clarify any points with the child
- audio or videotaping the interview and providing the transcript and/or tape to the solicitor acting for the accused or parent
- agreeing a joint interview or precognition by someone with experience in interviewing children which would then be accepted for use by all parties in subsequent proceedings
- establishing a group of experienced interviewers who were acknowledged to be 'honest brokers' with no affiliation to the prosecution, defence or other agencies.

The solicitors noted that there were frequent delays in receiving even a provisional witness list and thought that the procurator fiscal should ensure that the list of witnesses was attached to the indictment and served at least four weeks before the trial. Delays in service of the list meant that there was pressure to precognosce when the trial was imminent: 'If a full

---

[113] Following implementation of the Children (Scotland) Act 1995, guidance was developed addressing disclosure from the procurator fiscal to the reporter, in which discretion to disclose remained with the fiscal. In England and Wales, it is Crown Prosecution Service policy to disclose information to the local authority bringing child protection proceedings even if this may jeopardise the prosecution because 'the welfare of the child is of paramount importance'

disclosure of evidence is made at an early stage by the Crown then this may obviate the need to re-precognosce a child before the trial'.

Precognition by legal representatives in criminal or children's hearing court proceedings was not governed by any statement of good practice. Ten solicitors gave their views about what they considered good practice for precognition of a child witness. They all agreed that agents should carry identification when making a precognition visit and should visit by appointment only. The majority thought that it was good practice to allow a supporter to be present during precognition. Crown Office policy stated that the child's address should be listed as care of the police reporting officer.[114] However, only two solicitors thought that it was acceptable for them to contact the child in this way.

Policies concerning the conduct of the investigative interview[115] and medical examination[116] acknowledged the benefits to the child of the presence of a supporter. However, during Phase One of the study the policy on the presence of a supporter at the prosecution precognition were more restrictive. The Crown Office acknowledged that it may be appropriate for a non-witness supporter to accompany the child at the start of the precognition interview; however, in most cases the substantive part of the precognition should take place in the absence of the supporter who should be advised of this in advance. Whether the support person was allowed to remain was a matter for the precognoscer. A supporter whose presence was thought to be counter-productive could be excluded or the precognition delayed so that someone more suitable could be sought. In any case, the supporter should be warned not to prompt or seek to influence the child in any way.[117] In practice, procurators fiscal routinely precognosced young witnesses alone. Curators also said that they were advised to see children on their own. Reporters were more open to the presence of a support person during interview but agreed that the person should not be a witness.

PHASE TWO

The Interviews and Precognitions Pilot

The subgroup was chaired by a representative of the Scottish Children's Reporter Administration. Other members represented the Procurator Fiscal Service, Strathclyde Police, Glasgow Social Work Department and the Law Society of Scotland. This pilot aimed to address some of the problems identified in Phase One by assessing whether greater co-ordination and sharing of information could reduce the number of interviews of the child without compromising the rights of the accused. Because a definitive statement of inter-agency policy on investigative interviewing had never been published in a final version[118], the subgroup decided to focus on post-investigative interviews, particularly precognition.

---

[114] Book of Regulations 16.85
[115] Strathclyde Police (June 1993)
[116] Strathclyde Police (June 1995)
[117] Book of Regulations 16.87, 16.93
[118] The draft report "When Children Speak..." Report of a Working Group set up by the Secretary of State for Scotland and the Lord Advocate (1995)

From the outset, the subgroup acknowledged that neither the prosecution nor defence would forego their right to precognosce. However, one way forward was for the parties to give greater consideration to the purpose of a precognition or interview and that the pilot should highlight the need to be clear about the reasons for seeing the child, the options available and the possibility of using alternative sources of information.

The subgroup agreed the following 15 principles to meet the needs of both interviewer and child:

Statement of 15 principles of the Interviews and Precognitions Pilot

- a co-ordinated approach could limit the number of times child witnesses need to be interviewed
- a high quality of investigative interview, properly retained, together with appropriate updating and sharing of information could help to reduce the number of interviews
- those involved in the criminal or child protection investigation should address the information requirements of others in the system
- there can be different purposes of interview, i.e. for inquiries about evidence, rapport building, assessment and explanation. It is important for agencies and professionals to assess whether or not an interview is necessary for any or all of these purposes
- any person wishing to interview a child who has already been interviewed should be clear about their purpose in doing so and should consider alternative sources for the information required
- it is in the interests of all agencies and professionals that the child's evidence should be available and be uncontaminated and properly assessed (if necessary) before a case is heard in court
- assessment of the child as a witness is necessary for proper case management at court
- assessment of information and assessment of a child as a witness involve different skills
- the interview of a child requires a different approach from that for the interview of an adult witness
- when an interview is to take place, it should be conducted by someone with the appropriate skills
- repeated interviews of a child will contaminate the child's evidence
- repeated interviews may result in a loss of spontaneity and emotional response which in itself may affect a proper assessment of credibility
- while agencies and professionals ultimately have responsibility for the conduct of their own investigation and preparation of cases for court, the in-gathering of information, in particular the interviewing of a child, may be carried out by others outside that organisation or profession as long as the agency or profession has confidence in that person's ability
- agencies and professionals need to feel confident that they will not "lose out" by considering new practice and that different approaches may result in better information being obtained or assessments being made
- there should be an overview of the number and nature of interviews sought from a child witness and a person or persons should be specifically responsible for this overview.

The objectives of the subgroup

Drawing on the statement of principles, the subgroup agreed the following objectives for the pilot:

- to reduce stress to child witnesses and to preserve their evidence
- to minimise the number of times that child witnesses were asked to give an account of the alleged offence
- to minimise the number of interviewers
- to meet the information and assessment needs of all those involved in criminal and children's hearing court proceedings without re-interviewing the child about the evidence
- to identify and expand good practice without prejudicing the legal rights of any person affected by the process.

The subgroup prepared an information package to be given, along with the witness list, to those who might precognosce or interview children in pilot cases. It contained:

- information about the pilot and an explanation that recipients were not being asked to forego interviewing or precognoscing the child
- a good practice protocol for the conduct of precognitions, with an annex setting out alternatives to precognition
- questionnaires for completion before and after interviewing or precognoscing the child.

The protocol covering precognition practice addressed the choice of precognoscer, including the use of a specialist or a joint precognition; planning the precognition, including the location and who should be present; what information about the child is needed before precognition; and the need for a full and well-noted interview which may obviate the need for the child to be interviewed again. The annex discussed the problems caused by multiple interviews and considered alternatives to precognition. The package requested that participants review the good practice documents and record in the questionnaires their decision-making in relation to precognition in the case in question.

Precognition pilot objectives: to minimise the number of times that the child witnesses were asked to give an account of the alleged offence; to meet the information and assessment needs of all those involved in criminal and child protection proceedings without re-interviewing the child about the evidence; and to identify and expand good practice without prejudicing the legal rights of any person affected by the process

The subgroup's statement of principles identified the need for someone to take responsibility for an overview of the number and nature of interviews sought from a child witness. It planned that 'the professional actively involved with the witness at any given time' would maintain a central log of interviews, to be passed on, for example, from the police to the procurator fiscal. This attempt to require the police, procurator fiscal and reporter to track interviews other than their own proved unworkable. Even those described by the pilot protocol to be 'actively involved' with the child did not feel able to track interviews by other parties. Nor was there always a specific individual to whom the log could be passed, for example when the case was received in case marking at the procurator fiscal's office. The research team therefore assembled its own interview log for each child through information obtained from the police, procurators fiscal, reporters, social workers, solicitors and others. In some cases, the police permitted the research team to ask carers at an early stage to keep a note of requests to interview the child; this information was used to supplement information from other sources.

The eleven pilot cases involved 25 children. The following table shows how often they were spoken to about the alleged offences by the police, procurator fiscal, social workers (not including joint police – social work interviews) and solicitors:

Table 5: Number of times children were spoken to about the alleged offence

Interviewer	Number of times children were spoken to			
	Once	Twice	Three times	Four times
police	11	8	6	
procurator fiscal	8	6		
social worker	7			1
safeguarder			3	
curator			3	
reporter	2			
own solicitor	1			
defence solicitor	1			
doctor	4	2		
CCTV/ screens reports	6			
police exit interview at identification parade	11			
TOTAL	51	14	12	1

Taking these interactions together, the 25 children in this pilot spoke to someone about an aspect of their cases on average 4.76 times, ranging between one and 11 occasions. Ten of the children had spoken to someone five or more times. This did not include reports to friends, relatives or teachers who were usually the first people in whom the children confided.

By the end of the fieldwork, two children had given evidence in the criminal case and one at an application for a child protection order in the sheriff court. By the end of the pilot, further interviews were anticipated for seven children in the three cases which had not reached precognition and in which CCTV or screens applications might be considered. Instructions to those preparing reports supporting an application state that in order to minimise the number of times the child is interviewed, it should not be necessary to speak to the child about the application. However, the guidance also asks the author to address the child's preference about how to give evidence and it was clear from reading such reports that the authors had often discussed this with the child.

More detailed information was obtained for eight cases involving 16 children which had reached the stage at which precognition was considered.[119] Twenty-one pre- and 17 post-precognition questionnaires were returned. Fifteen had been completed by procurators fiscal or precognition officers, mostly from the child witness unit. Replies were also received from a reporter and three solicitors: two representing the child and her mother in children's hearing court proceedings and one from a defence solicitor in criminal proceedings. All respondents described themselves as experienced precognoscers. Their reasons given for wishing to precognosce were summarised as follows:

- a wish to assess the child's credibility and willingness to testify, to explore his or her current recollection and aspects of evidence not previously covered, and to build rapport (nearly all cases)
- to assess the need for CCTV or screens (two cases)
- to 'explore alternative explanations for the alleged offence' (given by both the procurator fiscal and defence solicitor in a case in which the children's versions of events altered over time).

In line with the pilot protocol which stressed the possibility of obtaining information from alternative sources, the pre-precognition questionnaire enquired about the extent to which this had happened. The prosecution reported seeking information before precognition from other sources about 11 of the 16 children: typically from carers, police officers, teachers or social workers. However, when prosecutors were asked whether any of the specific categories of information which they sought at precognition was available from such an alternative source, few said it was. Thus only one response stated that information on the child's competency was available from another source; four indicated that information on credibility was available and five said that information was available in relation to the child's willingness to testify. Nine conceded that the child's version of events was available from another source but only one respondent, a reporter, said that it would be possible to avoid asking the child to talk about the alleged offence during the interview.

All those who conducted a precognition and completed a questionnaire said that they had achieved the objectives specified in their pre-precognition responses. All prosecutors confirmed in post-precognition questionnaires that the child had been asked to talk about the offence.

---

[119] In the early stages of the pilot, it became necessary to abandon the subgroup's original plan that the package of good practice information and the questionnaires would be distributed by individual procurators fiscal. The paperwork was distributed instead by the research team as cases were identified

Defence precognitions did not feature significantly in this pilot. Crown precognitions had been disclosed or discussed with defence agent in four cases, one of which ended in a guilty plea. In the three remaining prosecutions, the defence requested access to statements. In two cases, no decision about disclosure had been recorded by the procurator fiscal. In the third, the fiscal did not offer disclosure but advised the defence to ask the police reporting officer to liaise with the families concerning the defence precognition. In that case, the defence precognosced one child but the other refused to cooperate. In the reporter's case, police statements were shown to the parents' agents prior to the children's hearing court proceeding. The procurator fiscal noted that he 'did not object' to disclosure by the reporter 'to avoid the child being precognosced'. However, the proof did not proceed and no precognitions by the parents' agents took place.

Precognition pilot objective: to reduce the number of interviewers

The number of different interviewers may add to the stress caused to children by multiple interviews. A change of police interviewers occurred in some cases where the first report was taken 'out of hours' by a uniformed patrol officer. Thereafter, where police officers interviewed in pairs or jointly with a social worker, at least one member of the original team was present if the child was seen again. Similarly, where social workers interviewed in pairs, one team member remained the same. Where the procurator fiscal precognosced more than once, the interviewer remained the same but this was not necessarily the same person conducting the trial. Children who were interviewed most had often spoken to at least seven different professionals. In one case in which there were children's hearing court proceedings as well as criminal proceedings, children spoke to two police officers, three social work personnel, the safeguarder, curator and members of the children's panel; precognition by the procurator fiscal was planned.

The pilot protocol suggested a number of alternative options to those contemplating precognition: asking someone who has already interviewed the child to interview again;[120] agreeing a joint precognition; and asking a 'specialist'. Precognoscers reported that none of these were feasible in the pilot cases. There was no sharing of information between the procurator fiscal and reporter in the three cases which involved both criminal and children's hearing court proceedings.

---

[120] In one of the other pilots, the procurator fiscal's case marking unit asked the police to interview a child again

Precognition pilot objectives: to reduce stress to child witnesses and preserve their evidence

In addition to addressing the number of interviews and interviewers, the question of stress to child witnesses was reviewed in three ways: by considering the extent to which supporters were used, the location of interviews, and soliciting the views of carers and others responsible for the children's welfare. The research did not assess the quality and methods of preserving the child's evidence. Police interviews with children were not routinely audio-taped. The question of videotaping had been considered in a previous enquiry.[121]

The interview location and whether a supporter could be present

Crown Office guidance stated that it may be necessary to have a number of meetings simply to gain the confidence of the child which may take place outside the office, for example at the child's home.[122] Reporters may also interview the child at home, school or 'some other place such as McDonald's'.[123] The pilot protocol suggested that the venue should be discussed with the parent/ carer because some children may not be comfortable with being interviewed at home. Responses to the pre-precognition questionnaire suggested that the carer was not routinely consulted about the location of the precognition. Ten children had at least one police interview at home but all children were precognosced at the office by the procurator fiscal. However, in one of the other pilots, two children with learning difficulties were interviewed at their school by the police and procurator fiscal.

The pilot protocol recommended that a supporter should be present during the interview or precognition; usually the parent/ carer, but where this was not appropriate an acceptable alternative should be arranged in advance. It was important to resolve the supporter's identity ahead of time because this person should not be a witness. A supporter was present with the child in 25 of the 45 police interviews in this pilot. The pre-precognition questionnaire asked whether the respondent had discussed with the child's carer whether someone should accompany the child during the precognition. All respondents said they would consult or had already done so.[124] However, it was the norm for the procurator fiscal to precognosce the child alone and a supporter was present throughout in only three of the 20 Crown precognitions.

The question about whether a supporter could be present at precognition was addressed in the booklet 'Your Child is a Witness' which was issued under the supervision of the Working Group. The advice in the booklet was carefully drafted to give advice that was even-handed to the defence and prosecution. The Group concluded that it was not appropriate to advise parents that they were entitled to insist on a supporter being present with the child during

---

[121] 'When Children Speak...' (1995) Draft Report of Working Group set up by the Secretary of State for Scotland and the Lord Advocate

[122] Book of Regulations 16.87

[123] Reporter to the Children's Panel, Strathclyde (2 March 1995)

[124] The standard procurator fiscal letter of invitation to parents states that 'The interview will be completely private and the interviewer will discuss with you whether it will be appropriate for you to be present throughout the taking of the statement from your child'

defence precognition, because it was procurator fiscal practice to interview children on their own. The booklet therefore could only advise that 'If the prosecution or defence ask to interview your child, you may *suggest* someone to accompany your child who is not a witness...' (emphasis added). Carers in this and other pilots spoke of the pressure they felt when asked for permission to question children on their own. Mothers spoke of feeling they had to agree with requests from the police and procurator fiscal to show they had nothing to hide. Police and prosecutors may have been unaware of the extent of the pressure felt. Subsequently, the Working Group was informed that a forthcoming amendment to Crown Office policy would reflect the assumption that a supporter should accompany the child throughout the precognition.

Precognoscers in the procurator fiscal's office spoke of the difficulties caused when supporters tried in a well-meaning way to prompt reticent children. The good practice protocol called for supporters to be advised about their role and its limits prior to the interview taking place. The procurator fiscal's child witness unit provided verbal advice but there were no written instructions for supporters at precognition.

The teacher who had acted as supporter during the investigative interviews of two children with learning difficulties later voiced regrets about taking on this role: 'The parents did not wish to be present in case it made the children uncomfortable. I was happy to sit in, thinking that I could keep things clear. I could see that the police did not understand T's account so I asked him to demonstrate the behaviour in question. At the trial, the defence accused me in my professional capacity of planting seed's in the children's minds and of contaminating their evidence. I left the witness box feeling intellectually damaged. In future, I would much rather stand back and not get involved'.

Views about the number and conduct of interviews

In order to build rapport with children and take account of their concentration span and what is known about their patterns of disclosing information, investigative interviews may need to be conducted over a period of time. Nevertheless, a reporter, social workers, a safeguarder and two mothers of young children expressed concern about the number of interviews in cases in which children were involved. The safeguarder noted that the Scottish Children's Reporter Administration's position, that safeguarders were not entitled as of right to see police statements, could sometimes necessitate additional interviews with children.

In the first case, children aged five and four were interviewed twice and three times respectively by the police. Their mother felt that the police interviews which lasted between half an hour and an hour were too long for her children, who were very upset afterwards. By the time of the four-year-old's third interview, his mother said 'he felt he was doing something wrong'. Both children were seen again by the police to 'check if they knew their numbers' for an identification parade which was cancelled at the last minute when it was decided to present identification evidence by other means. Their mother said: 'I was very relieved but in another way I was angry because they had gone through another interview and a test on their ability with numbers which there was no need for'. The four-year-old was precognosced twice by the procurator fiscal because of the child's short concentration span.

The mother concluded 'Something should be done about the number of interviews. It was a great relief when they were all over. It is traumatic enough for them to give evidence without having to be interviewed so many times'.

The second mother criticised the number of times her pre-school child had been questioned (twice by the police and twice by the procurator fiscal) as well as the apparent lack of co-ordination at the hospital where she reported the incident. The mother was asked to tell four people in succession what had happened; her child was with her in the same room and she felt that arrangements should have been made to keep the child out of earshot. After the final interview, she was given an appointment for the next day because there was 'no doctor available to attend to this kind of case'. She concluded: 'It was so confusing, all the build up to get there and get help and then I found myself outside the hospital just feeling stunned'. Following the Crown's precognition interviews, this mother described herself as 'really struggling' because the precognition had 'brought it all back up for me and my daughter. Afterwards she kept walking along with her head right down and a look of remorse. That's what I feel, putting her through it all again'.

In two cases, concerns were voiced about the timeliness of communications. In one, the report of a sexual offence was communicated to a social work department area manager on a Friday but the team dealing with the family was not notified until the following Tuesday. In the second case, a 15 year-old girl reported a sexual assault by her father to the police and was interviewed twice. Supporting statements were supplied by other members of her family. The social work department was notified on a Friday that the accused would be held in custody. The department apparently believed there was no urgency because they thought that bail conditions would be imposed if the accused was released. By the time a social worker visited at the beginning of the following week, the accused had been given a procurator fiscal's release from custody and was in the household again. No-one had warned the family that he would be released. When questioned by social workers in the presence of her mother, the girl withdrew the allegation against her father. She was not re-interviewed by the police but was seen four times by social workers in the presence of her mother. A case conference recorded that the mother was putting a lot of pressure on her child who seemed nervous and uncomfortable. The girl was removed on a child protection order five months later but only after telling her teacher that she wished to renew the allegations. This girl described herself as totally unsupported following her report to the police. She said:

> 'My dad carried on living in the house and warned us all to say he had moved out. The police officer never contacted me again after the interview. The police statement was the only time I ever told anyone what really happened to me. The social workers said they needed to get permission for overtime to come and see me because they had to come in pairs. That put me off. They asked to speak to me on my own but they asked me in front of Mum so I couldn't. They should have got me on my own and got the truth. They should have known I had to lie. They shouldn't have believed me.'

Carers generally praised the sensitivity of interviewers, though sometimes they considered that efforts to put children and carers at ease had not gone far enough:

> 'The police were nice but somehow they made me feel as if I was in the wrong' (mother)'

> 'My four-year-old was asked to call the precognoscer Mrs – this felt a bit cold and uncomfortable'.

In a case in which three children were interviewed three times by police and social workers because of inconsistencies in their reports, a social worker showed the research team the note of one re-interview of a nine year-old. The note opened with the police officer saying that people who tell lies can be sent to jail and asking the child 'Somebody is lying. Is it you?'. The social worker described the children as very upset about the number of interviews and this style of questioning. The curator said he was 'appalled' by these interviews and said that little had been achieved because the children changed what they said each time. In another case, the young witness recalled being upset at being asked to look straight into the police officer's eyes 'to see if I was telling the truth'.

It was important for the precognoscer for the Crown to be aware of any problems that arose during the police interview. In one of the support pilot cases, the child was able to communicate with the police officer during the investigative interview by writing things down and pointing to 'yes' and 'no' on pieces of paper. This technique was not used at precognition, where the child would not speak about the offence. The child witness officer discussed the use of special mechanisms for communicating with this child with the carer and precognition officer but the Crown Office decided that the case should not proceed before the precognition officer had an opportunity to try again. The police officer commented later that in her view the child would have been a competent witness.

EVALUATION OF THE CHILD WITNESS INITIATIVE

This chapter contains the results of the evaluation of the pilots described in the preceding chapters.

SUPPORT AND PREPARATION PILOT

Were the pilot objectives met?

The objectives of this pilot were:

- *to provide direct support, assistance and information to child witnesses*
- *to help them develop appropriate skills which would allow them to testify as fully as possible*
- *to create an opportunity for them to feel empowered by the experience of giving evidence*
- *to provide support and information to carers, assisting them to support children appropriately*
- *to help the child and family cope with the stress and anxiety associated with the witness role*
- *to communicate information about the child to others in the court process with the aim of ensuring that treatment of the child is appropriate to his or her needs and abilities.*

Additional objectives related to the role of the CWO:

- *to improve services to children and families in the pre-trial and court process*
- *to facilitate the flow of information in individual cases*
- *to raise awareness of good practice generally.*

The CWO was the means of delivering the objectives of this pilot. Favourable comments on the contribution of the CWO to the improvement of services and communication were received from professionals and carers, for example:

> 'The CWO played a vital role which was crucial for both my son and the family. She provided the missing link and gave us all the information and advice we needed' (parent)

> 'It was very valuable to have an independent person with an all round picture and information about what was going on, The CWO tried to pull all the disciplines together to get the best outcome for the children' (social worker)

> 'The CWO is brilliant! We found it really helpful. She brought books about court, played games with the boys and took us to visit the court. The kids really opened up to her and looked forward to her visits. If this role hadn't

> existed we really would have had no one and would have been told nothing' (parent)

> 'Without her we would have known nothing ahead of time' (carer)

> 'The CWO is a very good idea. It was important for my daughter that this was a woman. My daughter felt very at ease with her. She would have been in the dark and known nothing without the CWO' (parent)

> 'Most of the professionals involved have been really nice but the only person to pass on information or advice was the CWO' (parent)

> 'The CWO role is crucial, particularly in liaison with the school and family' (headmaster)

> 'This is a helpful role because even though we try to keep in touch with families, it's time-consuming and diverts effort away from case preparation' (procurator fiscal).

Liaison with the CWO was welcomed by teachers. They had the potential to play a key role in helping children; one girl who had contact with the police, social workers and reporter said of her teacher that he was the only person who supported her throughout. In cases in the other pilots, teachers often described themselves as marginalised:

> 'A mechanism should click into place automatically in these situations to manage the case, support the child and keep the communication flowing. It would have been helpful for M and the school to have had someone to communicate with'.

Start-up in the project was slow. Even though the CWO was only a part-time position and was unable to see all pilot cases through to completion because of the delay in referrals, children and families felt that she made a significant contribution on their behalf. Recent research has indicated that children who develop a trusting relationship with at least one system professional experience less trauma than those who do not have this opportunity.[125] Those whom the CWO supported felt markedly less isolated than other carers and children who were interviewed during the project.

The way in which the CWO functioned as a central point of advice was much valued. During the project, the CWO took part in a number of local presentations and training events for police, procurators fiscal, reporters, social workers and health professionals. As awareness of her position increased she received calls for advice and assistance from family members, social workers, procurators fiscal and lawyers about child witnesses in criminal, child custody and children's hearing court proceedings. There was little doubt that if the position

---

[125] J. Henry (1997) System Intervention Trauma to Child Sexual Abuse Victims Following Disclosure, 12 Journal of Interpersonal Violence 499

had continued, such requests would have increased in number. The research team also received many calls during the life of the project, indicating a demand for information and advice which was not readily being met elsewhere.

The remainder of the CWO's time was well used in brokering the development of the preparation protocol which the subgroup described as a 'valuable stand-alone document with lots of practical ideas and techniques that, with some training on their use, could be of help to anyone working to prepare a child to give evidence in court'. NCH Action for Children and Children 1st have agreed to publish the protocol.

Independence from other justice agencies was essential in establishing the CWO's credibility and objectivity. Co-ordination of information among agencies emerged as a substantial requirement of the position in addition to liaison with families. NCH Action for Children noted that 'trying to orchestrate agencies which are part of a powerful legal process is in itself stressful'. The CWO found the role of supporter in court to be particularly frustrating. These difficulties underlined the importance of appropriate line management and support for the CWO position. Information from child witness support programmes elsewhere also reflected the stressful nature of the work and the need for those conducting it to guard against feeling responsible for court outcomes.

In its report to the Working Group at the end of the project, the subgroup's key findings were that:

- the CWO position acted as a catalyst to ensure that the child's needs for preparation and support were identified and met by planning and implementation of a suitable programme
- structures were needed to identify child witnesses not just child victims
- preparation and support were not the remit of any one agency and there was confusion about who should take the lead in identifying the needs of the child
- resources were needed to provide other agencies with preparation and support skills
- procedures were needed to foster the communication of information about the child's needs and abilities.

The subgroup also identified multi-agency training needs relating to:

- passing on information about the child
- communicating with children
- preparing and supporting children at court.

Other findings

Carers throughout the pilots were often frustrated and angry that no-one had discussed with them or their children the alternative ways in which a child can give evidence. Crown Office policy stressed that applications for screens and CCTV should not be made routinely, but also emphasised the importance of the child's views in deciding what was best for the individual child.[126]

Most carers said that options had not been discussed with them; nor had anyone enquired in sufficient detail about the child's needs, abilities and concerns.[127] Many professionals appeared to assume that most children would be able to give evidence in open court, without checking with the children or carers. In certain cases, precognoscers were clearly reluctant to raise the possibility of screens or CCTV with the child and carer. One told the CWO that she did not want the options raised with the child 'in case it gave her ideas'. Another precognoscer told the researchers that 'there was no chance of screens because it was not a bad enough case' although the child had been permanently injured by the accused. Some parents said they were told that 'screens and CCTV were very hard to get'. For example, the carers of three seven-year-olds in a summary case confirmed that no-one had contacted them to ask about how their children should give evidence. One of these mothers who had wanted a screen said she had asked the defence precognition agent about it 'because, you see, we never saw anyone else'. At a pre-trial visit, one mother asked the precognition officer about the possibility of screens or CCTV, who replied 'We don't have them here, they're only in the High Court'. After the case was over, one of the parents in that case said: 'We never heard from the procurator fiscal about screens. How could people who know nothing about the court system know all the important questions to ask?' A 12-year-old said: 'I was feeling sick in the waiting room. I would definitely have wanted a screen or CCTV if someone had talked to me about it. I would have liked to have someone to talk to and tell me what to expect'. Another 12-year-old said 'I don't dream much but I wake up a lot at night. You should be able to insist on having a screen or CCTV. I'd tell them how scary it all is'.

The making of a CCTV application does not necessarily guarantee greater consultation with carers and children. In her study of CCTV use in Scotland, Kathleen Murray found that 91 per cent of parents wanted more of a say in the decision-making as to whether their child should use a special procedure. Only 35 per cent of children said they had any choice in the matter.[128] Australian research emphasised the significance of children's wishes in relation to the use of CCTV: their emotional well-being was influenced more by whether they were able to use CCTV when they wanted to rather than by whether they did or did not use it. Acknowledging the child's preference gave them a sense of control over the process.[129]

Those carers not supported by the CWO were frustrated and felt isolated when they experienced long periods in which they did not know what was happening. Lack of

---

[126] Book of Regulations 16.116
[127] Consistent with parental views expressed in K. Murray (1997) Preparing Child Witnesses for Court. Scottish Office Central Research Unit
[128] K. Murray op.cit.
[129] J. Cashmore and N. De Haas (1992) The use of closed circuit television for child witnesses in the ACT. Australian Law Reform Commission

information undermined the ability of carers to support their children.[130] Many were unsure whom to contact for information. Typical comments included:

> 'I wanted to ask about whether there would be a trial. I would have liked to see someone on my own'

> 'I wanted to find out what would be happening, what he was charged with, whether it would go to court. I couldn't get any answers. I still don't know'

> 'It would have helped a lot to have someone come out to talk to us and tell us what to expect'

> 'I tried everywhere to get some help but we were not a priority. You really shouldn't have to beg'

> 'No-one ever knew what was going on. It was awful. Most of our information came from the accused's family and it wasn't true but we didn't know it at the time'.

Carers' concerns included:

- whether the case would proceed
- uncertainty about the accused's bail or custody status
- uncertainty about the charges (some were still unsure about this even after the trial)
- decisions about how the child's evidence would be given and the options available
- lack of explanations for delays and for cases being re-listed to a later trial diet
- uncertainty as to whether a specific person could support the child at trial
- delays in receiving information about court outcomes.

Another major complaint concerned the amount of time that children had to wait at court and the number of children who attended and were sent away again. Taking the five trials in pilot cases together with 12 non-pilot trials observed in the course of the study, there were 22 instances of a child attending court for the purpose of giving evidence but not being called on that day. Such an event occurred in 10 of the 17 trials for which information was available. A young witness was sent away in one trial so that the sheriff could have time to practise on the CCTV equipment. Some children waited all day before being released and some did not give evidence until the third day of court attendance. In one of these cases, a child missed the first three days at her new school. The researchers were informed of another case in which two children travelled up from England on three occasions without giving evidence. On one of these abortive journeys they were contacted at Carlisle station to be notified of a change of trial date.

---

[130] K. Murray commented on the lack of information and support for carers. 'Parents were also conscious of their own limited knowledge and skill so that they were often at a loss to know how best to prepare the children'. Preparing Child Witnesses for Court (1997) Scottish Office Central Research Unit

The length of time that children wait at court can have a direct impact on the quality of their testimony. They may become tired, restless and increasingly nervous. Although there was a perception that older children aged around nine to 14 are better able to cope and less in need of special measures, this was not necessarily so. After a long wait, teenagers were often quickly upset by the courtroom full of people. Information from 13 trials indicated that, on the day on which evidence was given, children were at the court building for lengthy periods. Child witnesses in only four trials waited for less than two hours; the remainder waited for periods up to five hours. In one trial, a seven-year-old on medication for attention deficit disorder was the last witness called after a wait of over two hours. In another, a 13-year-old and his supporter were still at court at the end of the day having given evidence in the morning, because they had not been told they could go. Only one case appeared to use staggered arrival times for young witnesses.

There were also concerns about the waiting facilities, with a number of complaints about encounters with the accused or the accused's supporters in the court building. It seems that no young witnesses were brought into the building by a side entrance. Glasgow Sheriff Court's 'crèche' (a misnomer, as in fact it caters to children up to the age of 16) was established as a service 'directed to children who must be in court because they are the subject of a civil or criminal case or contested grounds of referral to a children's hearing or as witnesses in criminal cases'.[131] It is staffed by the Centre for Under-Fives Plus. Its co-ordinator reported that they used to receive a few referrals from procurators fiscal but even these had dried up, though she did not know why. Following the implementation of the Children (Scotland) Act 1995, fewer children needed to be produced at court for children's hearing court proceedings. Numbers of children using the crèche had fallen to 385 in the year to March 1998 from 658 the year before. The co-ordinator would have welcomed greater use of the facilities by the procurator fiscal and commented that children were 'only a phone call away' from any courtroom in the building to which they could be escorted on request. The crèche is open in the morning and with prior notice, staff keep the room open in the afternoon.

There were three instances in which carers had not understood the nature of the reporter's involvement. In the first case, the mother of a child who was injured by a non-family member said: 'I got a letter from the reporter which sounded scary and felt threatening. It said "We won't do anything this time"'.

In the second case, the accused was a taxi driver and the child victim had been unescorted because of education department policy. When contacted by the social work department on behalf of the reporter, the parents thought she was coming to offer counselling: 'Instead, she asked why we'd let my child travel alone and began talking about neglect and the at risk register and asked very personal questions about our past life and whether we owned our own home. I complained to the Director of Social Work and called the reporter but I never got an apology from the reporter'.

In the third case, the parent attended a children's panel hearing and subsequently received a citation to appear at the sheriff court because her child was deemed too young to understand

---

[131] Notice to Solicitors, Assistant Sheriff Clerk 23.5.1996

the grounds. At these hearings she said she kept trying to ask the reporter what was happening: 'We never got a straight answer that we understood. Later we got another letter telling us to go back to the panel where they discussed whether my child could stay with me or whether she needed supervision. This was the first time that we realised what was going on. Then they then said I could take her home'.

THE COMMUNICATIONS PILOT

Were the objectives met?

This pilot's objectives were:

- *to specify the nature of the information to be communicated about child witnesses, its sources, responsibilities for collecting and communicating the information, and the mechanisms for and timing of communication*
- *to ensure that information about the child flows through the system so that the child's needs can be addressed and decisions affecting the child's welfare can be made as early as possible*
- *to ensure that decision-making by the police, prosecution, reporter and judiciary can be well-informed.*

The subgroup set out in the protocol and checklist the information to be communicated about child witnesses. It also specified a wide range of sources for information about the child's needs, views and abilities. These included the child and carers, although in pilot cases they were not routinely referred to for such information. Other sources, including teachers and police officers who had observed the child's reactions at an identification parade, were also overlooked.

The triggering of procedures set out in the Lord Justice General's Memorandum depended on receipt of information about individual children. Despite this, judicial attitudes differed as to whether it was appropriate for sheriffs and judges to receive such information. There was no formal mechanism for the transmission of such information to those judges who were willing to hear about the child's needs.

The police had responsibility for collecting background information and communicating it to the procurator fiscal but the police report focused on the evidential basis for a prosecution and was not an effective vehicle for transmitting non-evidential information. An assessment of the child was seen as less pressing at the investigative stage, when it was not known whether the case would proceed. At the end of the pilot, the police indicated their willingness to consider the completion of a separate attachment or checklist about the child by the reporting officer.

Crown Office policy set out the procurator fiscal's duty to seek information about the child which was not already provided. Precognition prompted requests for information from carers but the results were not necessarily communicated to the court. The most effective mechanism for obtaining information and transmitting it to the court was the report commissioned by the procurator fiscal in support of applications for CCTV or screens. However, reports were prepared on behalf of only a small proportion of children. Where the advocate depute disagreed with the procurator fiscal's recommendation that an application be made, the reports were not used at court. There were few attempts to remedy information deficiencies in summary cases. Child witnesses in these cases were not precognosced and the procurator fiscal taking the trial was often assigned at a late stage. Even fewer children in summary cases were the subject of applications for screens or CCTV. Without information about the child's needs, views and abilities, procurators fiscal could not be confident that they had singled out those children most in need of statutory measures. In the study, some of the children experiencing significant distress pre-trial were involved in less serious cases.

Case discussions or conferences focused on child protection and despite the efforts of the pilot, did not share information relevant to the child's role as a witness. Nor was it possible to ensure that when relevant information was discussed, such as the impact of the alleged offence on the child or the supportiveness of the parents, that it would be communicated to the procurator fiscal. Similarly, background reports prepared for the reporter contained useful information about the child that was not necessarily passed on to the prosecution. Reporters said that it was not their responsibility to act as the 'middle link' or source of information for the procurator fiscal. The subgroup concluded that consideration of the checklist needed to be built into the structure of case discussions and conferences, with clearer guidance on to whom and by whom the information should be communicated.

Mechanisms for communication needed to ensure that information was updated and addressed the totality of the child's life. The research put together information from various sources about most child witnesses in pilot cases. It was striking that for many of them, involvement in the court process was only one disruptive or traumatic event out of several in their lives. Some had been witnesses before. Where abuse was alleged within the household, reporting to the police had often caused the break up of the family, resulting in relatives taking sides and rejection of the child in question. A number of mothers said they had been abused in their youth and said this affected how well they were able to support their children. Some children lived in chaotic home circumstances with parents who abused alcohol, drugs or were in prison. Several young witnesses experienced a change of carer or their family moved home while the case was pending - in two cases, because of house fires. Some had changed schools and one had been excluded from school. Another boy had suffered brain damage in a car accident. Children already in care had a change of key workers and in one case the children's home closed. Some children suffered the loss of a close relative. Such background information, as well as information about the anxieties related to the offence and the forthcoming court appearance, had a bearing on children's need for support, pre-trial planning and sensitive treatment at court.

The pilot cases illustrated ongoing problems of communication between therapists and procurators fiscal concerning the scope of pre-trial therapy.[132] The cases suggested that some children in need of special help did not receive it because of fears of contaminating their

---

[132] In her interviews with parents of Scottish child witnesses, Kathleen Murray documented a 'continuing lack of therapy and counselling' in the pre-trial period: Preparing Child Witnesses for Court (1993)

evidence. Some therapists were reluctant to begin work pre-trial. Others notified the procurator fiscal as required when therapy was contemplated, but were advised that even work focusing on the child's safety was inappropriate. Such advice seemed out of step with Crown Office policy that decisions about counselling were the responsibility of the child's carers and the procurator fiscal had no locus other than to advise whether the proposed counselling was likely to have an adverse effect on the prosecution.

The majority of forensic medical examinations in cases of alleged sexual assault were not conducted according to policy which recommended that examinations should be carried out jointly by specially trained physicians in suitably equipped hospital facilities. Information relating to the child's welfare was more likely to be communicated to the procurator fiscal and social work department if the examination was conducted by a hospital paediatrician. After the end of the project, a plan was initiated for joint hospital examinations of children under five by paediatricians and specially trained police surgeons.

THE IDENTIFICATION PILOT

Were the objectives met?

The objectives of this pilot were:

- *to introduce early contact between the police and the procurator fiscal to ensure that evidential issues in relation to identification are resolved, having regard inter alia to the means by which the child may ultimately give evidence at court*
- *to formalise good practice into a protocol for officers conducting parades and guidance on briefing child witnesses prior to the parade.*

Feedback from participants in identification parades indicated the importance of planning the child's involvement in the parade and preparation of the child and supporter for their roles. Towards the end of the project, the subgroup used the research findings to develop guidance not only for child witnesses and officers conducting identification parades, but also for the officer in charge of the investigation and the child's supporter. These checklists encouraged greater communication before and after the parade and were well received by police officers. Unfortunately, as no further identification parades took place before the project ended, there was no opportunity to evaluate the checklists or obtain feedback from children and supporters. The police plan to conduct their own evaluation of the checklists and to distribute them as good practice guidance for Glasgow.

Cases in the identification pilot were selected because of the decision to hold a parade. This decision took place at an early stage in five of the seven pilot cases, but was made as a result of inter-agency discussion in only four of these five cases. No consistent picture emerged of the basis for decisions concerning identification evidence in this pilot or in other pilot initiatives. Discussion at this stage between the police and procurator fiscal about how children might give evidence at court tended to focus on keeping options open for CCTV or screens applications rather than asking carers about the needs and preferences of individual children about how to give evidence. In a few cases in other pilots where CCTV applications were an option, it was decided that identification evidence could be provided by someone other than the child and no parade was necessary.

Shifts in procurator fiscal policy on identification parades and dock identification occurred at the start of the pilot as a result of interpretation of case law. Changes were not disseminated consistently and appeared to add to confusion rather than reducing it. Police views differed from those of procurators fiscal; individual interpretations varied widely. Police officers were concerned for child welfare and resource reasons at the prospect of parades being required automatically for greater numbers of child witnesses than previously even where the accused and the child were related. Some sheriffs did not expect a parade to be held in such cases.

Following discussions of tentative pilot findings at the end of the project, further guidance was issued by the procurator fiscal which clarified the categories of cases in which parades were necessary and those in which they were desirable. It was confirmed at that time that an identification parade was not a prerequisite for a CCTV application.

Other findings

Despite the issuance of further clarification of procurator fiscal policy, by the end of the pilot the subgroup had not made significant inroads on its underlying concern of avoiding unnecessary distress to young witnesses by reducing the need for them to identify the accused. Children and carers were mistakenly assured that participation in a parade would mean that the child would not need to identify the accused at court and children were therefore not prepared for the possibility of a dock identification request.[133] Previous Scottish research identified 'being taken by surprise on the day of trial' as 'one of the worst experiences for the children and parents.'[134] Looking at the accused, whether at a parade or when asked to make a dock identification, is upsetting for many children. Policies in effect at the end of the project suggested that an increasing number of children may be asked to do both. Early discussions were needed to find out the views of the child and carer in order to inform decisions about identification evidence.

Children were frightened by the closeness of the line-up through the one-way screen and the contrast between the brightness of the parade room and the darkness of the witness room. Witness suites in other forces visited during the study used larger rooms which allowed greater distance between the witness and the line-up, and which did not require lighting to be dimmed on the witness side of the one-way screen.

The subgroup explored two ways of further reducing the trauma of children attending identification parades: video-recording the parade and showing it to the witness at some later point[135] and allowing the witness to view the parade over a CCTV link. A police

---

[133] Crown Office policy states that children should be told that they will be asked to point out 'who is responsible' Book of Regulations 16.105

[134] K. Murray (1997) Preparing Child Witnesses for Court. Scottish Office Central Research Unit

[135] Research suggests that identification performance at live and videotaped line-ups is 'virtually identical': B. Cutler et al (1989) Eyewitness Identification from Live Versus Videotaped Line-ups. Forensic Reports, Vol. 2, 93 - 106

demonstration of both options was arranged for subgroup members and this proved helpful in raising practical issues. The subgroup acknowledged that further work needed to be done and that the resource implications were considerable. Provisions for showing the witness a videotaped parade already exist in England and Wales under the Police and Criminal Evidence Act 1984. Over 20 English forces are evaluating a computer database of video clips. The witness is shown a videotape of seven people comprising the suspect and six others chosen by the suspect from the police database. This system is believed to reduce stress for witnesses, save resources and greatly increase the range of 'stand-ins'.[136]

The subgroup report to the Working Group concluded that its original objective, to examine the options to reduce the use of dock identification at court, remained valid but its achievement was dependent on legislative reform. It recommended that the topic be referred for consideration by the Scottish Law Commission.

THE PRECOGNITION AND INTERVIEWS PILOT

Were the objectives met?

The objectives were:

- *to reduce stress to child witnesses and to preserve their evidence*
- *to minimise the number of times that child witnesses were asked to give an account of the alleged offence*
- *to minimise the number of interviewers*
- *to meet the information and assessment needs of all those involved in criminal and child protection proceedings without re-interviewing the child about the evidence*
- *to identify and expand good practice without prejudicing the legal rights of any person affected by the process.*

Crown Office policy acknowledged the need to avoid multiple interviews with child witnesses. Rather than relying on the investigative interview and other sources of information in petition cases, procurators fiscal felt that it was essential that the child be interviewed again, though not necessarily by the lawyer conducting the trial. This responsibility was often delegated to a precognition officer.

Defence lawyers in pilot cases were willing to forego precognition provided that the prosecution disclosed the child's evidence. The prosecution turned down a defence request for disclosure in only one case and this resulted in the sole example of a defence precognition in this pilot. Experience in other pilots suggested that the defence was more likely to precognosce in summary cases. Such interviews were usually carried out by agents for the defence lawyer. One solicitor, after arguing that the defence's right to precognosce was essential, added 'Of course I wouldn't do the precognition myself'.

---

[136] The Times, 3 November 1996

The pilot was not successful in having the police, procurator fiscal and reporter track interviews other than their own with the child. An overview of the total number of times each child was interviewed was only possible by putting together information from different sources. Only one of the 25 children in this pilot was interviewed once. The average number of interviews was 4.76 per child, with three children having been interviewed 11 times. These figures did not take account of precognitions which had still to come in unfinished cases. For some children, multiple interviews were seen as very stressful.

One of the pilot objectives was to reduce stress for child witnesses. This included limiting the overall number of interviewers. Options suggested in the pilot protocol to achieve this objective were not used. A supporter was present in just over half of the police interviews but in only three out of 20 precognitions conducted by the procurator fiscal. It was unclear whether children were asked if they wanted a supporter present, but carers felt under pressure to agree to let children be interviewed on their own.

The case of Anderson v HM Advocate 1996 SCCR 114 was raised during subgroup discussions. This case was sometimes cited by defence solicitors to justify precognition of Crown witnesses, even after disclosure of a witness's evidence from the procurator fiscal. That case established that the circumstances in which the conduct of the accused's legal representative will provide a ground of appeal 'must be defined narrowly and that the conduct must be such as to have resulted in a miscarriage of justice'. This ruling did not appear to preclude consideration by the defence of some of the alternatives to precognition proposed but unused during the pilot.

THE RESOURCE IMPLICATIONS OF THE PILOT PROJECTS

The cost of alternative CWO models is discussed in the report of the Working Group.

Estimating the number of child witnesses requiring support and preparation was handicapped by the lack of information about numbers in the system. Rhona Flin's study of child witnesses in Glasgow in the late 1980s suggested that approximately 1,440 witnesses aged 15 and under were cited over a 12 month period, though only 31 per cent of the total actually appeared in court.[137] Kathleen Murray's CCTV research found that 19 per cent of High Court cases had one or more children under the age of 16 cited as witnesses (486 children over a 27 month period beginning in 1991, a total which included Edinburgh as well as Glasgow cases).[138]

On behalf of this study, at the beginning of 1996 the Glasgow procurator fiscal's case marking unit identified 246 witnesses aged between four and 16 in police reports received over a four week period. Multiplied up, this suggested an annual rate of almost 3,500 children. Given that only a small proportion of cases reported to the police are likely to be prosecuted, this would still suggest that several hundred children are cited annually in criminal proceedings in Glasgow. The Scottish Children's Reporter Administration agreed to

---

[137] R. Flin et al (1990) The Child Witness. Report to the Scottish Home and Health Department
[138] K. Murray (1997) Preparing Child Witnesses for Court. Scottish Office Central Research Unit

monitor the number of child witnesses in reporters' referrals in Glasgow beginning in April 1998 but no figures had been supplied at the time of writing this report.

In projecting the scope of services for children appearing at court, those appearing in relation to civil matters, including custody disputes, should not be forgotten. Although there are apparently no official statistics, it is considered that the numbers of such children had increased since the implementation of the Children (Scotland Act) 1995.[139]

In the identification pilot, there were significant cost and resource implications for an increase in the number of parades in child witness cases. The Scottish Office and Strathclyde Police were unable to provide an estimate of unit costs, but the elements included:

- the time taken to organise the parade
- preparation time with the child witness, possibly including an advance visit to the parade suite
- transportation costs for witnesses and payments to stand-ins
- accommodation costs
- the time of officers attending, including the CID officer conducting the parade, verifying officer and officers to debrief and take exit statements from witnesses
- preparation of the identification report to the procurator fiscal.

Conversely, there are potential savings to made under these headings if the number of identification parades involving child witnesses can be reduced.

In the communications pilot, the subgroup concluded that the resource implications of the pilot arrangements, though not measured, were not significant:

> 'The problems thrown up are not necessarily those which are best solved by additional resources in any event, but rather better co-ordination and more effective use of existing resources'.

However, there are resource implications for the introduction of standard police child witness checklists and procurator fiscal child witness reports.

The precognitions and interviews subgroup did not address the question of the costs of implementing its proposals. However, a reduction in the total number of interviews of child witnesses could result in savings for the police, procurator fiscal and Scottish Legal Aid Board. The wider issue of disclosure of police statements and Crown precognitions also has significant resource implications and is apparently the subject of current review:[140]

The pilot findings had significant implications for inter-agency training but this would require a separate exercise to determine the costs.

---

[139] R. McKay 'Are Our Courts Child Friendly?' The Herald Magazine 2.5.1998
[140] 'Scots lawyers fear new shift in policy' The Herald 4.2.1998

EVALUATION OF THE PROCESS BY WHICH THE WORKING GROUP DEVELOPED AND IMPLEMENTED THE PILOT INITIATIVES

The task undertaken by the Working Group was daunting. The needs of child witnesses touched on sensitive issues which cut across agency boundaries. The Group spanned a period of nearly four years and this made changes in its membership unavoidable, a problem compounded by major local government reorganisation and other key organisational changes which took place during the lifetime of the Group. Only the chairman was continuously involved with the Group from its inception. His commitment was a key factor in identifying and maintaining a coherent vision of the Group's objectives.

There were also changes over time in the agencies represented. The lack of a judicial representative in the early stages was a significant drawback, remedied when a sheriff joined the Group in its final year. Others joining during the course of the project included representatives of the medical profession, the courts, Victim Support and NCH Action for Children.

The range of organisations represented was a strength which enabled a truly multi-agency perspective to be achieved during discussions. The Group was also unusual in the breadth of its scope which encompassed criminal and children's hearing court proceedings and children who were witnesses, not just victims. Participants often remarked that Group meetings provided a unique opportunity for inter-agency exchange and their effectiveness in this respect was contrasted with previous experience of Child Protection Committees prior to local government reorganisation. The Group acted as a 'clearing house' for topical concerns and provided a forum in which members could raise and sometimes resolve issues round the table. Meetings allowed inter-agency links to be established between individuals at a level where normally there was no direct contact. One member commented that prior to the Group's formation, when staff wanted to raise inter-agency concerns they had to go 'up the ladder' to a more senior person who would decide whether to take it up with his counterpart in the other organisation, 'and then it would take time for the answer to filter down again'. This collateral benefit from the work of the Group continued throughout its existence and was one of its most successful aspects.

The Group was a vehicle for raising awareness among practitioners of ideas from other jurisdictions. Examples included visits by Group members to child witness support projects in England, attendance at a course on prosecution of child abuse in the United States and consultation with police forces in England and Wales on the use of video in connection with identification parades.

The Working Group sought to fulfil its brief in Phase Two of the project through the pilot subgroups. Membership was drawn exclusively from the Working Group and many representatives were called upon to sit on more than one subgroup. While this ensured good communication between the groups, it placed a significant burden on members for all of whom involvement in the initiative was additional to their normal duties. As a result, it was often hard to achieve progress at meetings because of the absence of one or more key individuals. The lack of continuity of representation affected the subgroups, only one of which had the same chair person throughout. Changes in representation often brought different interpretations of agency policy. This sometimes resulted in the re-opening of issues already debated at length and on which an agreed position had previously been reached.

When the subgroups were set up, the researchers produced briefing papers covering the objectives, outputs and methods of each pilot. There was a danger that they would take on too much responsibility for informing the work of the pilots. Although the researchers were aware of this problem, the boundary within which 'action research' operates proved to be a fine line. The involvement of the Scottish Office Central Research Unit at Working Group meetings was essential in policing this boundary.

Despite delays, all subgroups generated pilot protocols with a multi-agency perspective which could be tested in the pilot cases. Documentation was produced to inform practice. The subgroups were less successful at disseminating information about the pilots and persuading those involved in pilot cases to follow the proposed procedures. During fieldwork, the researchers frequently encountered a lack of knowledge about the Group or its activities even though briefing material describing the pilots had been given to each of the agencies and professional groups involved. There was little evidence that this information had reached its target audience. An article to raise awareness among the legal profession was still pending as the close of the project approached.

Some problems about 'delivery' of subgroup messages may have related to the level at which agencies were represented on the Working Group. When it was first set up, some organisations nominated a senior policy representative as well as a senior practitioner. By the time the subgroups were underway, some of the senior policy people had withdrawn. The 'hands-on' knowledge of the practitioners in developing the pilot protocols was essential, but they were less well-placed to deliver an agency commitment to implement pilot objectives. The police were an exception in that both levels of representation were maintained through the project. For the future, a more effective structure might be subgroups of practitioners reporting back to a Working Group of senior managers with authority to disseminate information and commit their staff to new procedures.

In conclusion, the Working Group and subgroups, with their focus on young witnesses, not just victims, proved effective in raising and exploring inter-agency concerns for which no alternative forum was available. For example, the differing interpretations by the police and the procurator fiscal of the circumstances in which an identification parade was required may not have been identified and addressed so quickly if not for the Group's oversight. The Working Group was also effective at developing guidance requiring an inter-agency perspective. Examples included the preparation and support protocol, to be published by NCH and Children 1st; the booklet 'Your Child is a Witness' published by Strathclyde Police; four guidance documents for police officers, children and carers about identification parades; and guidance on the child's attendance at court, produced by the Scottish Court Service.

However, agencies were not obliged to comply with practice advocated by the Group. A comprehensive training strategy will be needed to achieve the changes in attitudes and culture identified during the research. Implementation of the Working Group's recommendations will require compliance to be monitored and agencies to be held accountable for their performance in providing support services to young witnesses.

CONCLUSION

UNDERLYING PRESUMPTIONS ABOUT THE TREATMENT OF CHILD WITNESSES IN SCOTLAND

The Lord Advocate's aim in setting up the Working Group on Child Witness Support was 'to improve arrangements for the support and preparation of child witnesses'. Its remit included the formulation of proposals for the dissemination of good practice on a national basis. This study took place in Glasgow but the Working Group considers that its conclusions are likely to be valid elsewhere in the country.

The Group's terms of reference emphasised the need for the arrangements to 'respect the best interests of the individual child'. The Group took as its starting point the Scottish Law Commission's statement in 1990 that young witnesses could give evidence 'by conventional means without suffering undue trauma or stress' provided that they received 'careful pre-trial preparation... coupled with sensitive handling of the child from the moment of arrival at the court house'.[141] Crown Office child witness policy is founded on the belief that most children will be able to give evidence in open court with 'appropriate support' and, if necessary, with procedural modifications such as those described in the Lord Justice General's Memorandum. Applications for the statutory options of screens or CCTV are considered appropriate only in 'exceptional circumstances'.[142]

There is an underlying assumption in these policy statements that the system will make adequate provision for the needs of most child witnesses so that only a few will require special measures. This assumption is predicated on:

- child witnesses and their carers being routinely advised about alternative ways to give evidence[143]
- systematic communication about the needs, abilities and fears of all child witnesses to those making decisions about the presentation of the child's evidence
- a screening process which treats consistently those children for whom procedural modifications and statutory options are appropriate
- account being taken of the views of the child[144]
- the provision of 'careful pre-trial preparation', 'appropriate support' and 'sensitive handling' for child witnesses in general.

The picture presented by this study, both in evaluation of pilot cases and from the wide range of interviews conducted over the past three years, suggests that none of these premises is well-founded. Children and carers are not routinely consulted about the best way for the child

---

[141] Para. 1.8
[142] Book of Regulations 16.121
[143] In order to express a view 'the child will require information in relation to the available options': Book of Regulations 16.116
[144] Section 271(7) Criminal Procedure (Scotland) Act 1995

to give evidence; indeed, even when they raise questions about eligibility for CCTV and screens they may not be able to get an answer. Information about the child is not routinely gathered, passed on, or requested if not supplied. Background reports about the child's needs are prepared only after a preliminary decision to make an application for CCTV or screens. This makes it impossible to draw an accurate picture of the extent of the needs and capabilities of child witnesses in general.

The views of professional participants as to children's abilities to cope often differ from those of the children and their carers. While it is true that many young witnesses appear unaffected by their court involvement, many others are deeply distressed even though this is not always apparent in the courtroom. Trauma is not related exclusively to the nature or seriousness of the offence. Without routine feedback from children, their carers and those supporting them, the claim that the current system allows most young witnesses to give evidence 'without suffering undue trauma and stress' cannot be substantiated.

When the Scottish Law Commission reported in 1990, it considered the appointment of someone to prepare child witnesses for court, provide continuous support and 'to protect and perhaps represent' their interests. Although the Commission decided against recommending a new position for this purpose, it urged those involved in existing arrangements to develop 'new and improved ways to protect the child's interests'.[145] This study has examined the provision of support and preparation for young witnesses before court and the management of cases in which they give evidence. It has found few examples of the sensitive handling and innovative procedures envisaged by the Commission.

THE WAY FORWARD

The research role in this project provided a unique opportunity to observe and contribute to the Working Group's deliberations over a period of more than three years. The Group created a unique forum in which agency perspectives could be explained, problems could be ventilated and alternative solutions discussed. It set an ambitious agenda for its pilots and if they did not succeed in all they attempted, nonetheless they acted as a proving ground in shaping the way for future child witness developments. The pilots produced a range of examples of good practice as well as a salutary illustration of the difficulties of implementing change across complex organisations. Although the Lord Advocate's Working Group itself has come to an end, its members wish to continue to meet periodically because of its value as a local forum.

The way forward needs to take account of Articles 12 and 13 of the UN Convention on the Rights of the Child which guarantee the child's right to impart information:

> 'There is an obligation not only to hear a child witness but to free the child from any constraints or fear, anxiety or distress which might inhibit his evidence. The Convention creates an obligation to create the optimum

---

[145] Para. 5.4

circumstances in which a child as witness is freed to give his or her account of events'.[146]

Implementation of the Working Group's proposals requires services for child witnesses to be taken forward by means of an integrated structure, taking a holistic view of children's experiences in the justice system and of the organisations with whom children come in contact. This integrated approach is implicit in the package of recommendations agreed by the Group. The proposals are closely inter-related. Addressing the issues in isolation is unlikely to achieve a significant improvement.

In 1997, the government set up parallel working groups in Scotland and in England and Wales on the treatment of vulnerable or intimidated witnesses in the criminal justice system. The English interdepartmental group reported in June 1998.[147] The Scottish group's report 'Towards a Just Conclusion - Vulnerable and Intimidated Witnesses in Scottish Criminal and Civil Cases' was published by The Scottish Office in November 1998. It recommended 'that the findings of the Working Group on Child Witness Support be used to inform improvements in support for child witnesses, once its work is complete.'

Strategic implementation of the Working Group's package of recommendations as a whole would again put Scotland in the forefront of child witness policy and practice. Such action is essential in order to fulfil the commitments about the treatment of child witnesses on which current policies concerning child witnesses in Scotland are based.

---

[146] A. Cleland and E. Sutherland (1996) Children's Rights in Scotland. W. Green/ Sweet and Maxwell
[147] 'Speaking Up For Justice'. Home Office

ANNEX A

Address to the jury in cases in the sheriff court involving a child witness

In this trial, evidence may be led from child witnesses.

At the end of the trial, when you retire to consider your verdicts, you will have to consider the evidence of any child witness in exactly the same way as you consider the evidence of the other witnesses.

As with each witness, whether adult or child, it will be for you – and you alone – as sole judges on matters of fact, to decide what evidence you accept as being both credible and reliable and what evidence you regard as being either false or unreliable. You can accept a part of the evidence of a particular witness – whether an adult or a child – as being both credible and reliable but reject another part of that witness's evidence because you regard it as being false or unreliable.

These decisions are entirely matters for you and nothing to do with me.

My responsibility is to ensure that the trial is conducted fairly and properly in accordance with the law. It is my responsibility to explain the law that is relevant in this trial and to direct you upon that law.

It is also my responsibility to ensure so far as is reasonably practicable that the experience of giving evidence by any child witness causes as little anxiety and distress to the child as is possible in the circumstances.

To that end, it is necessary to take steps to put any child witness at ease and to minimise distress and anxiety to that child.

Accordingly, you will find that my approach in respect of a child witness will be different from my approach to an adult witness. That is simply because of my responsibilities in respect of any child witness.

My approach in respect of any child witness will be an open and friendly approach designed to put the child at ease whilst giving evidence.

But I wish to emphasise to you and to state clearly to you that nothing in my approach to or dealing with any child witness is intended to indicate in any way to you any view which I may form as to the credibility or reliability or otherwise of that child witness.

It is not for me to indicate to you any view which I may have as to the credibility or otherwise of any witness – adult or child – and I shall not do so.

So you must not take from my dealings with any child witness any sort of supposed indicator of my views on that witness.

Any child witness, whether truthful or untruthful, reliable or unreliable, in her evidence or any part of her evidence must be treated properly by me so that the experience of giving evidence causes as little distress as is possible in all the circumstances, because at the end of the day the child is a child.

Since the coming into force of s 56 of the LR (MP)(S) Act 1990 evidence of a child can be authorised to be given by means of a television link. It may be that this will happen in this trial. In that event, the child witness must not come into the courtroom and you will see and hear the child witness on a television screen.

Any such evidence forms part of the evidence in the trial and you will have to consider such evidence in exactly the same way as you consider all the other evidence put before you. You should know that when a child gives evidence by means of a television link that child will not see you. The child will only see me or the person who is asking the child questions at a particular time.

As you can appreciate, it is sometimes necessary with child witnesses to interrupt their evidence to give them a break or a rest or to go to the toilet and if that is necessary here then that will be done.

ANNEX B

The Lord Advocate's Working Group on Child Witness Support: Report and Recommendations

FOREWORD

The Working Group on Child Witness Support was established by the Lord Advocate in January 1995 with the aim of improving arrangements for the support and preparation for court of child witnesses. In Scotland a child is defined as someone under the age of 16 years. The Working Group initially considered extending its deliberations to young witnesses up to the age of 18 and even 21. While the Working Group fully acknowledged that chronological age was not always the significant indicator of vulnerability, for practical purposes the focus of the Group's deliberations centred on those under 16.

The Lord Advocate's remit for the Group was:

- to consider arrangements to support children affected by criminal or children's hearing court proceedings and identify necessary improvements

- to design, implement and evaluate a pilot initiative in Strathclyde over a period of two to three years

- to commission research to assess child witness arrangements

- to formulate proposals to disseminate good practice on a national basis.

The Working Group operated according to the following principles:

- the arrangements to support child witnesses would respect the best interests of the individual child

- each child would, in the first instance, be assumed to be capable of giving evidence in the conventional manner

- the arrangements would respect the necessary confidentiality of each agency

- arrangements would require to obtain the confidence of those responsible for the representation of accused persons and parties to children's hearings.

The Working Group's overarching concern was to improve the support of children without jeopardising the rights or responsibilities of others in the court process. It also wished to see an enhancement of practice in relation to all child witnesses across the full range of legal proceedings. The Group believes that the scope of this initiative, encompassing both criminal and children's hearing court proceedings, is unique in the UK.

Although the Group drew on information and research from the widest possible field and, indeed, members visited child witness support projects in Surrey, South London and

Humberside, the Working Group focused its main enquiries about practices and procedures and its pilot initiatives to the Greater Glasgow area. The Group met on 28 occasions and was chaired by the Crown Office. Initial membership of the Group was drawn from Strathclyde Police, Glasgow Procurator Fiscal Service, Strathclyde Social Work Department, Strathclyde Reporter to the Children's Panel and Law Society of Scotland.

The Scottish Office Central Research Unit was invited to sit on the Group to provide necessary professional guidance in relation to the Group's remit to commission research but also for guidance in the identification and interpretation of other relevant research. The Group is grateful for the assistance which the Central Research Unit has provided throughout the four years of its deliberations. In particular, the guidance provided by Joe Curran, Susan McVie and Fiona Fraser has been invaluable. Between them, they attended most of the Group's meetings and ensured that the Group made best use of the research which was commissioned, with the aid of The Scottish Office, to support and inform the work of the Group.

Following selective competitive tender, Joyce Plotnikoff and Richard Woolfson were commissioned through The Scottish Office's criminal law research vote to support the Working Group by providing research based advice, monitoring the work of the Group and evaluating the pilot initiatives designed to influence local practice. The Group could not have been better served and a unique and symbiotic professional relationship was formed between the researchers and the Group. Joyce Plotnikoff and Richard Woolfson are recognised experts in their field and provided invaluable objective knowledge and advice, often under severe time constraints. With the assistance of the Central Research Unit, they were able to maintain objectivity while being sensitive to the processes of negotiation and compromise which the Group had to adopt.

As a result of organisational changes during the course of the Working Group's lifetime, social work representation was provided by Glasgow City Council Social Work Department and Reporter representation by the Scottish Children's Reporter Administration. In addition, membership was extended to include representation from the Sheriffs' Association, NCH Action for Children, Children 1st, Victim Support Scotland, Scottish Courts Administration, the Scottish Court Service, Yorkhill Hospital (consultant paediatrician) and Strathclyde Police (Chief Medical Officer).

A full list of members, both past and present, is provided in an annex to the Working Group report. As chair of the Working Group, I want to thank them all for the time and attention they gave to the work of the Group, not only in regularly attending meetings of the Group in Glasgow but also in attending meetings of the pilot groups to which they were attached and preparing papers. Particular thanks are due to NCH Action for Children and Children 1st for funding on a part time basis a child witness officer and to Strathclyde Police for publishing and distributing a leaflet devised by the Group for parents and carers called 'Your Child is a Witness'.

Sadly, two members of the Working Group (Fiona Bevan, SCA and Donald MacDonald, Strathclyde Police) died during its course. I and the rest of the Working Group and research colleagues missed their expert advice and pass on our condolences to their families.

I should also mention the Group's unanimous view that interaction within the Group was a considerable benefit on a day to day basis and that a permanent forum was required. These feelings are reflected in our first recommendation.

L A HIGSON
Aberdeen, March 1999

THE LORD ADVOCATE'S WORKING GROUP ON CHILD WITNESS SUPPPORT

Introduction

Scotland has long been in the vanguard of innovative studies concerning child witnesses. In 1986 Rhona Flin and Graham Davies were commissioned by what was then the Scottish Home and Health Department to study young witnesses and identify the sources of stress for them in criminal proceedings. That project, based in Aberdeen for two years[148] and in Glasgow for a further two years,[149] was believed to be the first study of its type in the UK.

In 1986 the Lord Advocate referred the law governing children's evidence to the Scottish Law Commission. It published a discussion paper in 1988 along with a research paper prepared by Kathleen Murray who reported on alternatives to in-court testimony in criminal proceedings in the United States of America. The Commission Report on the Evidence of Children and Other Vulnerable Witnesses was published in 1990 and was followed by legislation giving effect to its principal recommendations.

In 1992, the Scottish Office commissioned Kathleen Murray to evaluate the use of the live television link for child witnesses in Scottish trials.[150] The research report was published by the Central Research Unit (CRU) in 1995. In 1997, CRU published her review of the literature and a survey of practice in England and Wales.[151] Her report included an analysis of parents' and children's perceptions about CCTV and going to court in Scotland. The views of children and parents are a crucial aspect which has tended not to form part of similar research in other parts of the UK.

The Working Group's Programme

The work carried out by the Working Group was divided into two broad phases, each supported and informed by the work of the research team of Joyce Plotnikoff and Richard Woolfson.

Phase One

During Phase One, which ran from October 1995 to March 1996, the Group reviewed professional practice and procedures in the Greater Glasgow area in relation to child witnesses in criminal cases and in relation to children appearing in proof hearings referred from Children's Hearings to the Sheriff Court. This involved examination by the Group of practice regarding police identification and interviewing procedures for child witnesses; it also involved an in-depth look at interviews of child witnesses carried out by other agencies such as the procurator fiscal, the defence solicitor, social workers and voluntary organisations. Procedures for the communication of information to children were examined. Medical practitioners' examinations

---

[148] R. Flin et al (1988) The child witness. Report to the Scottish Home and Health Department, Edinburgh
[149] R. Flin et al (1993) Child witnesses in Scottish criminal trials. International Review of Victimology, 2, 309-329
[150] Live Television Link: An Evaluation of its Use by Child Witnesses in Scottish Criminal Trials
[151] Preparing Child Witnesses for Court

and interviews of child witnesses were also scrutinised. In addition, child witnesses' experiences of court were studied in order to achieve a broad overall picture. In detail, the Group set itself the tasks of:

- mapping current professional practice, structures and relationships, and identifying examples of good practice

- identifying the needs of child witnesses

- identifying mechanisms for the improvement of practice and procedures and a transitional path for putting such improvements into practice

- producing a plan for a pilot initiative

The Research team was crucial in taking forward these tasks and was commissioned, with the active co-operation of the relevant agencies, to examine policy and practice documents and to interview practitioners. In the event, the researchers conducted 130 interviews and produced a detailed working report which greatly assisted the Group by providing objective support to the range of knowledge of its members about the strengths and weaknesses of current practices in relation to child witnesses. The findings from this phase of the research are covered in the researchers' report which forms part 2 of the current document.

Phase One Conclusions

The review identified a wide range of child witness policies in which certain good practice principles were common to all organisations. Nevertheless, the overall picture suggested that only certain categories of young witnesses were likely to receive adequate support, and that responsibilities for support, liaison, information flow and monitoring were poorly defined.

There was a need to bring elements of good practice together into an *integrated child witness support structure* which would augment the services available to young witnesses without undermining the existing roles and responsibilities of individual organisations.

The Working Group concluded that the building blocks of such a structure should include:

- documentation which made clear the child witness policies and procedures of individual organisations

- agreements between organisations to co-ordinate procedures in relation to young witnesses

- codes of good practice for the legal profession

- guidance describing the scope of appropriate support and preparation of the child for court

- explanatory materials for young witnesses and their parents or carers[152]

- information for the judiciary about young witnesses

The researchers had suggested that one key to the creation of an integrated child witness support structure was an independent child witness support officer (CWO) to act as a central point for information and advice for those working directly with young witnesses, and who would also prepare for court some children who would not otherwise receive this service. The Working Group concurred. NCH Action for Children and Children 1st agreed to fund an experimental CWO position on a part-time basis for one year during Phase Two of the work of the Group.

Phase Two

The second phase of the Working Group's programme began in April 1996. Five pilot initiatives were established to take forward the identified aspects of the proposed child witness support structure. These pilots were:

- **Support and Preparation of Young Witnesses for Court.** This involved an examination of comprehensive preparation programmes to properly support child witnesses without risking contamination of evidence, equipping young witnesses with the confidence and skills needed to render their evidence to the court.

- **Child Witness Officer.** This involved consultation with the various agencies to define the independent role of the CWO in relation to preparing young witnesses, checking their understanding of the court proceedings, and addressing their interests and anxieties about the proceedings both pre- and post-trial.

- **Young witnesses' identification of the accused.** Alternative methods of identification evidence were examined in order to reduce stress for the child witness.

- **Communication within the Legal Process of Information about the Child Witness.** A protocol was drawn up and a checklist sent to inter-agency case discussions; sources of information were identified; the passing on of the information in order to ensure that the necessary decisions are made as to the child's welfare was also looked at; to ensure that all legal agents are well-informed.

- **Interviews and Precognitions.** The pilot explored the number of times child witnesses were asked to discuss the circumstances of the alleged offence; a protocol was set up regarding precognition practice; questionnaires were administered to practitioners and children and their carers were interviewed about stress caused by multiple interviews.

---

[152] The Crown Office booklets 'Going to Court as a Witness?' for the age-groups five to 12 and 12 to 16 were published in 1998

The research team was commissioned to:

- support the sub-groups for each of the pilots

- establish the extent to which the pilot initiatives met their objectives

- assess the resource implications of implementing the initiatives on a wider scale

- describe the role played by the organisations involved and the extent to which the best practice applied in the pilots varied from normal practice

- ascertain the views of practitioners and (where appropriate) children and their parents or carers about their experience

- evaluate the process by which the Working Group developed and implemented the pilot initiatives

Pilot subgroups, drawn exclusively from members of the Working Group, were identified to steer the pilots and to report back to the main Group. Each subgroup was tasked with developing an action plan and protocol stating the pilot's objectives and the practice to be followed by participants. The research team supported the development of the pilot initiatives by preparing discussion papers drawing on recent developments in published and unpublished child witness research and practice in England and Wales and elsewhere. Towards the end of the project, each subgroup submitted a working report to the Working Group.

A small number of cases was identified for each pilot to test the feasibility and efficacy of the proposed new practices and procedures. Small number were considered appropriate both to avoid imposing too heavy a burden on participants who were being asked to adopt new procedures and to allow the cases to be studied in detail. By the end of Phase Two, 26 cases involving a total of 66 children had been monitored by the research team and 190 interviews had been conducted. These case studies enabled the researchers to evaluate the process of implementing change across the pilots. In addition, they observed 32 young witnesses in non-pilot cases giving evidence at court.

Phase Two Conclusions

Identification of even a small number of cases to be monitored during the pilots proved relatively difficult, illustrating a particular problem in establishing a more integrated structure for child witness support. The Group concluded that crucial aspects of such a system would be a coherent and integrated inter-agency policy on the identification and prioritisation flagging of child witness cases, the sharing of information, the publication of statistics on such cases and a mechanism to coordinate and organise these aspects, to ensure that support and preparation are provided where necessary.

The Working Group concluded that more needed to be done in relation to guidance and training to establish a uniformity of good practice in relation to child witnesses, both inside and outside the courts.

Despite a great deal of research evidence about the often large number of interviews which many child witnesses experience and the potentially detrimental effect which they may have on the child, the research team found that children in the pilot studies often experienced multiple interviewing. While the Group recognised that agencies found it difficult to identify ways in which they might forego interviewing a child witness, it concluded that more should be done to improve the quality of such interviews, including precognitions, and to share information derived from them.

Ways should be explored to reduce the stress for young witnesses in relation to the identification of the accused.

More guidance and training is required in relation to familiarisation visits of child witnesses to courts.

Clarification is required in relation to the nature and timing of pre-trial therapy for child witnesses.

More needs to be known about children's hearing court proceedings (proof hearings)[153].

It was found that in the majority of sexual assault cases forensic medical examinations were not conducted according to policy and best practice. The Working Group concluded that, in order to comply with policy, forensic medical examinations should be carried out jointly by specially trained physicians, i.e. by paediatricians and specially trained police surgeons, in suitably equipped hospital facilities.

There is a need for a more consistent approach to be taken towards child witnesses by the judiciary.

While recognising that there is a growing body of information available, the Working Group concluded that a way needed to be found for publishing and distributing the booklet for parents and carers - 'Your Child is a Witness' and that similar materials were required in relation in relation to proof hearings.

The Working Group does not underestimate the difficulty of the task of developing an integrated child witness support structure. While the Working Group worked hard to reach agreement over the practices and procedures tested out through the pilots, some negotiations were delicate and certain compromises difficult to sustain. Nevertheless, the achievements of

---

[153] Where the Children's Panel wishes to go ahead with a case, but the grounds of referral are not accepted by the parents and child, or are not understood by the child, the hearing must direct the reporter to apply to the Sheriff for a finding as to whether the grounds for referral are established; The Social Work (Scotland) Act 1968 s42 (2) and s42 (7); The Children (Scotland) Act 1995, s65 (7) and s65 (8)

the Working Group serve to demonstrate what can be done with inter-agency co-operation and with a clear focus on the needs of child witnesses.

During its four years of work, the Group produced four guidance documents:

- on identification parades for police officers, children and carers

- the Child Witness Officer's protocol on the support and preparation of young witnesses for court

- guidance for court personnel on the child's attendance at court, produced by the Scottish Court Service

- the booklet for parents and carers entitled 'Your Child is a Witness' which was published by Strathclyde Police

Copies of these documents can be obtained, from Mrs Betty Bott, Crown Office, 25 Chambers Street, Edinburgh.

Towards the end of the lifetime of the Working Group, two important and relevant consultation documents were issued. The first was the report of the Working Group on Vulnerable and Intimidated Witnesses entitled 'Towards a Just Conclusion'. One of the recommendations in the report is that the findings of the Child Witness Support Working Group be used to inform improvements in support for child witnesses. The other report was that produced by the Scottish Courts Administration (SCA) on 'Measures to Support Child Witnesses'. The SCA plan to conduct a further consultation exercise on compellability of children and once this is complete to put together a package of reforms relating to children who give evidence in court.

RECOMMENDATIONS OF THE WORKING GROUP

The Working Group believes that it has successfully fulfilled the remit set for it by the Lord Advocate in 1995. Throughout the four years of its work, the Group considered in great detail arrangements for the support of child witnesses and has identified and sought to test out, through a series of pilot exercises, improvements to those arrangements. Crucial to the work of the Group was the support and objective assessments of the research team. Finally, many of the recommendations which follow, not only identify what the Group considers to be necessary improvements to practices and procedures but they also represent proposals for the dissemination and implementation of good practice on a national basis.

The Working Group's recommendations have been organised under the following headings and each set of recommendations is preceded by an account of how the Working Group arrived at its conclusions. The headings are:

- Taking forward an integrated child witness support service

- Achieving a more consistent approach by the judiciary

- Improving communication about young witnesses and planning before the trial or children's hearing court proceedings

- The communication of information to the judiciary about individual young witnesses

- Good practice on the questioning of young witnesses

- Prosecution practice and policy

- Improving the quality of investigative interviews and the sharing of information to reduce the number of time the child is questioned

- Identification evidence

- The child's familiarisation visit to the court

- The child's rights and pre-trial therapy

- Children's hearing court proceedings

- Publications

- The need for statistics about young witness cases

Taking forward an integrated child witness support service

The remit of the Working Group required it to design, implement and evaluate a pilot initiative. In Phase One, the researchers proposed a model structure for an integrated child witness support service, underpinned by a series of policy and practice documents and with the position of independent child witness officer (CWO) as its keystone. The model acknowledged organisations' existing responsibilities to young witnesses but aimed to enlarge the scope of service provision and make it more consistent. This concept was endorsed by the Working Group and aspects of the model were taken forward through a series of pilot initiatives in Phase Two.

The CWO combined the delivery of support services to children and carers with the task of communicating their needs to other agencies. The liaison aspects of the role were appreciated by the organisations involved, being described both as a catalyst and, in a constructive sense, as a professional irritant. The CWO was uniquely placed to assess policy effectiveness, the quality of inter-agency co-operation and the management of individual cases. The feedback she provided to the Working Group was a valued feature of its meetings. The CWO experiment was considered by the Working Group to have been successful.

A number of the documents regarded as vital components of the initiative were produced during Phase Two but the Group concluded that the structure also required an implementation strategy to address areas where reform would not be accomplished simply by the revision of policy or the production of guidance.

The Working Group considered how the role of CWO might be taken forward and in what form. It seemed that child witness support was a responsibility shared by several agencies but owned by no one. Without a specially designated role, delivery of service would continue to be limited to the provision of a familiarisation visit to the court, and even this would be available to a relatively small proportion of young witnesses. There would be no broad accountability for practice which failed to comply with individual or inter-agency policy.

Two Working Group members and the CWO visited NSPCC child witness projects in Surrey and South London which were staffed by social workers. Working Group members also visited a child witness project in Humberside, based on an inter-agency collaborative model which appeared to be of greater relevance to circumstances in Scotland. It was launched in 1995 by the former Humberside Child Protection Committee and continued after local government reorganisation in 1996 under the auspices of the new Area Child Protection Committee (ACPC) for Kingston-Upon-Hull and the East Riding of Yorkshire.

The Humberside project is run by the Child Witness Co-ordination Group, a subgroup of the ACPC chaired by the ACPC manager. The Co-ordination Group members include ACPC agencies as well as representatives from courts, the Crown Prosecution Service and voluntary agencies. This multi-agency structure has reportedly led to a feeling of joint ownership by those involved and eased the task of inter-agency liaison which is a crucial component of the child witness support role.

The scheme has approximately 60 child witness familiarisation workers drawn from professional staff in ACPC agencies (social work staff, teachers, police officers, health professionals and representatives of voluntary child care agencies) which contribute the staff time required and mileage costs. The workers receive training on multi-agency child protection work, the signs and symptoms of abuse and child witness preparation and support. For cases that do not go to trial, workers spend approximately six to ten hours with the children; in trial cases, this increases to around 15 to 25 hours. Where possible, cases involving several children are assigned to familiarisation workers within one member organisation, such as a family centre.

The Humberside scheme covers inner city and rural areas whose total population is estimated to exceed 560,000, of whom approximately 130,000 are children. The Co-ordination Group has set up systems with the police, prosecution and courts to identify child witnesses at an early stage in order to assess their needs and track case progress. The number of young witnesses identified by these tracking systems has surprised the agencies involved. In the first year of operation, July 1995 to June 1996, there were 447 referrals. Following local government reorganisation which entailed a reduction in the catchment area, the service received 349 referrals between April 1996 and March 1997. This rose to 455 referrals for the year ending in March 1998, an increase of 39 per cent on the previous year. The Co-ordination Group describes its monitoring role as essential to its work:

> 'One cannot quality assure a service without good quality data. We have discovered over a period of three years providing this service that the provision of a good quality, accountable service cannot be provided without resources'.[154]

The Co-ordination Group liaises with local judges and undertakes training with Crown Prosecution Service caseworkers and magistrates. In addition to its annual report, it also provides a report giving feedback from children and familiarisation workers about aspects of the system which worked well and those which were seen to need improvement.

Costs of the Humberside scheme for the year 1997/98 amounted to £35,000 which covered the salary of a full-time co-ordinator and administrative support. These costs were met partly by the ACPC and partly through joint funding for three years from health and social services. The costs did not include office accommodation which was provided by social services. NCH Action for Children has advised the Child Witness Support Working Group that, based on its experience of managing the CWO position, future costs of a full-time child witness officer and administrative support are likely to be closer to £39,000 per annum.

The community-based Victim Support scheme and the court-based Witness Service are members of the Humberside Child Witness Co-ordination Group but do not provide familiarisation workers for the child witness project. These voluntary organisations feel unable to provide the necessary skills or resources to deal effectively with the needs of child witnesses.

---

[154] Response dated August 1998 of the Kingston-Upon-Hull and East Riding of Yorkshire ACPC Child Witness Service to the consultation paper "Speaking Up For Justice"

A Scottish Office evaluation of pilot witness support schemes run by Victim Support concluded that the schemes provided a valuable service.[155] The Scottish Office consultation paper 'Towards a Just Conclusion' recommended that, subject to the availability of resources, the witness support pilots should be extended to as many sheriff courts as possible.[156] It might therefore seem logical to suggest combining the volunteer-based service for all witnesses with a service for young witnesses. Although the Working Group considered that a Victim Support witness service could assist with familiarisation visits and waiting arrangements for young witnesses, the Group concluded that this would not be an appropriate mechanism for delivery of a specialist service for young witnesses in Scotland. It was notable that many young witnesses monitored during the research for the Working Group had experienced other stressful events in the pre-trial period, not all of which were related to the case itself. Some children were described as traumatised by offences which were not considered serious by the legal process. In the Victim Support pilots, most contacts with witnesses were brief and over half lasted for under ten minutes. The child witness support responsibilities envisaged by the Working Group include in-depth pre-court preparation work, tailored according to an assessment of the child's needs, and liaison with justice system agencies. The Working Group has concluded that these functions are best carried out by trained child witness supporters with relevant professional experience.

The Working Group is reluctant to propose the creation of a new structure and considers that Child Protection Committees are the logical vehicle for the delivery of an independent child witness support service. However, some members of the Working Group have expressed reservations about the appropriateness of the Child Protection Committee in its existing form to take on operational responsibility for child witnesses.

Recommendation 1: that in order to provide support services for young witnesses in a structure providing greater consistency and inter-agency accountability:

1.1 Child Protection Committees should appoint a subgroup to take forward operational support of young witnesses with terms of reference covering both criminal and children's hearing court proceedings and young witnesses in general, not solely those who are victims. Subgroup members should represent all key groups, including the judiciary

1.2 child witness officers should co-ordinate independent familiarisation services provided by trained employees of Child Protection Committees' member organisations. In less populated areas, this co-ordinating role may require only a part-time or shared position

1.3 those involved in child witness support and preparation should receive training on the standards set out in the protocol developed by the Child Witness Support Working

---

[155] D. Lobley and D. Smith (1998) Victim Witness Support in Scotland. Scottish Office Central Research Unit
[156] Towards a Just Conclusion: Vulnerable and Intimidated Witnesses in Scottish Criminal and Civil Cases (1998) Scottish Office

Group, which describes the scope of appropriate preparation and emphasises the need to avoid doing anything to contaminate the child's evidence

1.4 Child Protection Committee member agencies should contribute the time of staff acting as familiarisation workers, mileage and training costs and accommodation for the child witness officer, as in the model adopted by the Child Witness Co-ordination Group, a subgroup of the Area Child Protection Committee for Kingston-Upon-Hull and the East Riding of Yorkshire

1.5 The Scottish Office should be invited to consider options for resourcing child witness officer co-ordinators and the necessary administrative support, including the possibility of partnerships with child welfare organisations. It is estimated that coverage of the 26 Child Protection Committees for Scotland could be achieved for £663,000 (based on £39,000 for a full-time co-ordinator with administrative support in eight Child Protection Committees, with the remaining 18 Committees being served by 18 half-time positions)

Achieving a more consistent approach by the judiciary

Judges and sheriffs in Scotland, unlike many of their counterparts in England and Wales, are generalists and do not receive any special designation or 'ticket' enabling them to preside in serious sexual assault, child witness or family law cases. Most members of the judiciary in Scotland encounter child witnesses infrequently and have little opportunity to find out how their colleagues manage such cases. It is therefore not surprising that there were wide variations in the exercise of judicial discretion in relation to child witness cases. The Scottish Law Commission hoped that the issuance of judicial guidance would promote 'some desirable uniformity of approach' in judges' treatment of child witnesses[157] and as a result of its recommendation, guidance was issued in 1990 as the Lord Justice General's Memorandum. The research found that, despite the Memorandum, it was still impossible to tell young witnesses with any certainty about the measures to be adopted at trial. Unpredictability was also a feature of children's hearings court proceedings. The Commission had hoped that judges would be as sensitive as possible to the need to put children at their ease; it was aware that 'many judges are already alive to this need, but we suspect that some may not be'. The research found many instances of judicial good practice but also examples of judicial insensitivity.

In 1996, Paul Cullen, QC, the then Solicitor General, said that 'it was time to revisit the Memorandum' which was issued before the legislative provisions requiring the court to take account of the views of the child witness in deciding whether to grant an application for CCTV or screens.[158] The research findings suggest to the Working Group that a Memorandum on its own is not an adequate vehicle to deliver the 'desirable uniformity of approach' called for by the Commission.

---

[157] Report on the Evidence of Children and Other Vulnerable Witnesses (1990)
[158] Scottish-American Conference on Protecting Children, Scottish Police College, Tulliallan 28.8.96

Phase One of the research suggested that guidance for the judiciary should be developed that would promote a more consistent approach to the management of child witness cases in Scotland.[159] Specific examples were considered, particularly the Child Victim Witness Manual commissioned by the California Center for Judicial Education and Research[160] and written by a lawyer and psychologist. This has been described as containing 'a wealth of advice on the management of cases relating to children properly founded on a critical review of the relevant psychological research and practice'.[161]

Commenting on this research proposal, Sheriff Iain Macphail, QC described the provision of such guidance for the judiciary as 'a difficult matter'.[162] While he agreed that 'there is everything to be said for lawyers keeping themselves well-informed' he was also of the view that 'it would be objectionable if a judge were to reach a conclusion by supplementing the evidence and submissions before him with his private knowledge of some relevant topic'. The question of the judge's personal knowledge has since been addressed by the Honourable Lord Sutherland dismissing an appeal on grounds that the sheriff, in assessing the witness, took into account his own private research into the subject of sexual abuse:

> 'As far as his references to the literature were concerned, what the sheriff was doing was not commenting on the reliability or credibility of the witness. What he was commenting on was the issue as to whether a failure to complain at the time had any bearing on the credibility and reliability of the witness as to the substantive facts which were in issue. On one view it could be said that the sheriff was conferring an advantage on the defence since he was giving them due warning at a very early stage in the case that this would be something which would be exercising his mind at the end of the case'.[163]

Gaps in the understanding of judges and other criminal justice personnel in England and Wales in respect of vulnerable witnesses were identified in the 1998 report 'Speaking Up for Justice' which emphasised the importance of bridging these gaps:

> 'To be effective, the content and format of training programmes must be appropriate to the needs of those people it is designed to assist (i.e. vulnerable or intimidated witnesses) and this is best achieved by consulting with expert organisations'.[164]

---

[159] Guidance for the judiciary on children now includes material in a 'starter pack' for new High Court judges; a session on child witness and child welfare issues in induction courses for new temporary and permanent sheriffs; up-date seminars for permanent sheriffs in 1998-99; and showing the NSPCC video 'A Case for Balance', demonstrating good practice when children give evidence, at Scottish judicial studies seminars. Letter from Sheriff Charles Stoddart, Director of Judicial Studies in Scotland, 24.7.98

[160] E. Matthews and K. Saywitz (1992)

[161] J. Spencer and R. Flin (1993) The Evidence of Children, Blackstone Press

[162] Sheriff Iain Macphail, QC 'Child Witness Support Initiative: A Response' (1997) Socio-Legal Research in the Scottish Courts. Vol. 4 Scottish Office Central Research Unit

[163] B v Ruxton, 1998 Green's Weekly Digest 24-1191

[164] Paras. 12.1 and 12.9, Report of the Interdepartmental Working Group on the treatment of Vulnerable and Intimidated Witnesses in the Criminal Justice System. Home Office

'Speaking up for Justice' recommended that a steering group carry out a costed training needs analysis of its recommendations, along with the development of co-ordinated guidance and training templates and incorporating specialist knowledge of vulnerable witness issues.[165]

Recommendation 2: that in order to promote the 'sensitive handling' and 'desirable uniformity of approach' advocated by the Scottish Law Commission in its 1990 Report on the Evidence of Children and Other Potentially Vulnerable Witnesses:

2.1 the Scottish Courts Administration should consider the production of good practice guidance for judges and sheriffs on the management of young witness cases. Development of this guidance and training should take place in consultation with organisations that have specialist knowledge of young witness concerns

2.2 the Lord Justice General should be invited to consider revision of his Memorandum and how to raise awareness of its provisions among the judiciary and practitioners

2.3 the Scottish Court Service, in consultation with the Lord Justice General, should consider conducting a pilot to assess the feasibility of allocating criminal and children's hearing court proceedings involving young witnesses to nominated and trained members of the judiciary

Improving communication about young witnesses and planning before the trial or children's hearing court proceedings

One of the pilots aimed to improve communication within the legal process of information about young witnesses. The pilot developed a 'child witness checklist' which identified categories of background information including maturity, abilities, language development, health concerns and the child's views about going to court. Such information was needed at an early point to inform key stages of case processing and planning for the management of the case at court. However, the pilot was less successful at identifying processes to collect and pass on this information.

The Lord Advocate's Guidelines to Chief Constables require the police to include 'full information' about the child in their reports to the procurator fiscal in cases which may be eligible for use of one of the statutory measures, but there was no prescribed format for doing so and police reports studied by the researchers generally did not contain this level of detail.[166]

---

[165] Para. 12.17

[166] In England and Wales, the standard confidential witness information form MG 6 used by the police to provide information to the Crown Prosecution Service requires the police to record specific information about young witnesses

The research also found that case discussions and case conferences within the social work department's child protection procedures did not deal with child witness issues.[167] One department representative concluded that the research had revealed 'rather patchy understanding of the needs of child witnesses' and the importance of 'assessment of this need being enshrined in the routine processes and structures of the department'. Greater efforts were needed to alert carers to the importance of passing on and updating information about the child to decision-makers in the legal process. The communications pilot subgroup took the view that there were training implications for all the organisations involved but most subgroup members thought that implementation of systematic procedures for the communication of information would not require significant additional resources. The reporter representative, however, considered that meaningful implementation would require considerable additional work.

Recommendation 3: that in order to ensure information about young witnesses is available to inform decision-making in the legal process:

3.1   systematic procedures should be developed by all those involved in the criminal justice process and children's hearing court proceedings to gather and record background information about the child witness. This is likely to require the development of special forms and the revision of case discussion and case conference procedures

3.2   multi-agency training should emphasise the important contribution of background information about the child to planning for the trial or children's hearing court proceedings and the management of the child's evidence at court

The communication of information to the judiciary about individual young witnesses

The Lord Justice General's Memorandum invited judges to take each child's particular circumstances into account, including their maturity and any special factors concerning their disposition, health or physique before deciding what steps, if any, should be taken to minimise anxiety or distress while giving evidence. However, the research found that there was no formal opportunity for communicating this information to the judiciary and indeed several judges and sheriffs were circumspect about receiving it.[168] The communications pilot subgroup suggested

---

[167] The project 'Support for Child Witnesses in Hampshire' examined the minutes of over 100 child protection case conferences in order to obtain information about children entering the criminal justice system. It found that the minutes 'contained practically no references to criminal proceedings, even though one might reasonably speculate that there would be some overlap..'. Draft report (1998) NSPCC Practice Development Unit

[168] In England and Wales, a pre-trial plea and directions hearing is held in all Crown Court cases. A standard checklist, 'the judge's questionnaire', is filled in by advocates on both sides before the start of the hearing; the judge completes the remainder with any orders concerning pre-trial planning. The judge's questionnaire contains some questions relating to child witness cases. A supplementary checklist is to be introduced exclusively addressing child witness issues including the use of a supporter, the time of the child's attendance at court and stand-by waiting arrangements, the child's special circumstances and the arrangements to be made to accommodate them

that the judiciary could, with advantage, receive a limited subset of information from the child witness 'checklist', filtered by the procurator fiscal or reporter, in the form of a child witness report.

At the end of the pilot it was still uncertain precisely which categories of information should be provided to the judiciary. The Council of the Sheriffs' Association was therefore invited to comment on the child witness checklist, and to highlight those items concerning a child witness which it was appropriate to communicate to the sheriff and at what point in the proceedings. The Association supported the proposals for improved communication in the interests of particular children but commented that there were 'very many cases where children give evidence about events such as road traffic accidents where their accounts are simple factual narrative' when it would be unnecessary to make enquiries about the child's circumstances.[169] While it was appropriate to communicate 'legitimate information, e.g. that a child witness has a hearing difficulty', the Association emphasised that the sheriff must not be informed of perceptions of the child's credibility or reliability. There was no difference between the information that could be made available in sheriff and jury trials and in summary trials.

Judges and sheriffs often found out just before trial that a case involved a child witness, making it impossible to plan in advance with any degree of certainty. Some sheriffs interviewed during the project thought that information about the child and matters relating to the child's testimony, such as time of attendance at court, questions about identification evidence and the identity of a support person, should be raised with the defence at an interim diet. However, even though it was generally agreed that first diets (in solemn procedure cases) or intermediate diets (in summary cases) should be used to plan how child witness cases would be dealt with, this seldom happened.[170] A further weakness was the lack of a pre-trial planning meeting in High Court cases. However, in one pilot case, the trial sheriff held a planning meeting in chambers a few days before the trial. The procurator fiscal and defence solicitor attended this meeting. Deciding various administrative matters in advance of the trial was felt to have greatly aided the taking of the evidence of two young children.

Some sheriffs who were interviewed for the research felt that information about the child witness should be submitted in writing, rather than relying on the sheriff at an interim hearing making a note for the court file. In contrast, the Sheriffs' Association considered that a written report was appropriate only in exceptional circumstances, where the child was 'in an unusually sensitive position e.g. a health problem', when a note could be passed up by the procurator fiscal with the consent of the defence just before the child entered the courtroom. Otherwise, information need only be communicated orally by the procurator fiscal before the child entered

---

[169] Responses from Sheriff Brian A. Lockhart, Honorary Secretary, Sheriffs' Association, 31 August 1998 and Sheriff Ian A. Cameron, Convenor of Council Subgroup, 5 September 1998

[170] 'Special factors relevant to the child, if disputed, should have been capable of resolution with the assistance of responsible counsel or solicitors at a first or preliminary diet... such diets are not yet being used as extensively as they could be for the discussion and resolution of such matters'. Sheriff Iain Macphail, QC 'Child Witness Support Initiative: A Response' (1997) Socio-Legal Research in the Scottish Courts. Vol. 4 Scottish Office Central Research Unit

as 'a report prepared in advance is liable to be mislaid or overlooked'.[171] This problem was confirmed by some sheriffs in interview who were concerned that reports supporting applications for CCTV or screens, which often contained information relevant to the management of the child's evidence (for example that the child had learning difficulties or a short attention span), were not always included in their trial papers.

The Working Group concluded that there was a need for written information to be supplied to preliminary hearings to facilitate case management and consideration of the Lord Justice General's Memorandum. If the position of child witness officer is introduced, this person could assist in compiling the necessary information and reports.

Recommendation 4: that, in order to prompt consideration of provisions in the Lord Justice General's Memorandum and to facilitate case management decisions:

4.1 a format should be agreed for a written child witness 'report' for sheriffs and judges, to be provided by the procurator fiscal or reporter at a preliminary hearing where possible, and its implications discussed with the sheriff and defence or other agents

4.2 the Scottish Court Service should ensure that the child witness report and reports in support of CCTV and screens applications are available to the trial judge or sheriff

4.3 where possible, the sheriff to conduct the trial or children's hearing court proceeding should be identified beforehand and invited to convene a meeting in chambers with the parties before the day of trial or children's hearing court proceeding to decide matters relating to the child witness

4.4 in order to ensure continuity in the provision of information to the courts, the Lord Justice General should be invited to investigate the practicality of regulating the procedures for communicating information about young witnesses to the judiciary at interim diets, by way of Act of Adjournal

Good practice on the questioning of young witnesses

During the research, many interviewees (including social workers, procurators fiscal, reporters and family members) expressed great concern about the way in which the questioning of children at court was conducted in certain cases, and the inconsistency of the judicial approach to intervention when cross-examination was perceived as oppressive. The Scottish Office consultation document on vulnerable and intimidated witnesses notes that the court has inherent power to prevent inappropriate or intimidating cross-examination and recommends that 'appropriate opportunities be taken to emphasise the court's role in preventing inappropriate or intimidating cross-examination'.[172] Judicial guidance should elaborate on the circumstances in

---

[171] Responses from Sheriff Brian A. Lockhart, Honorary Secretary, Sheriffs' Association, 31 August 1998 and Sheriff Ian A. Cameron, Convenor of Council Subgroup, 5 September 1998

[172] Para. 5.7 and Recommendation 14, 'Towards a Just Conclusion' (1998)

which intervention is appropriate; examples are available from other jurisdictions.[173] Some judges have found that the setting of basic ground rules out of the presence of the jury (for example, emphasising the need to avoid repetitive questions, questions with double negatives, multiple questions or questions combined with assertions) has made it easier to identify when lines are crossed and questioning is deemed to have become inappropriate.[174]

Recommendation 5: that in order to improve the standard of questioning of young witnesses:

5.1   the Lord Advocate should consider inviting all those involved in criminal and children's hearing court proceedings to collaborate on the development of guidance on the questioning of children in court

5.2   the Director of Judicial Studies in Scotland should be invited to refer to such guidance in judicial training, in order to develop a more consistent approach to judicial intervention when questioning is deemed inappropriate

Prosecution practice and policy

The research identified a number of instances in which the treatment of young witnesses at the sheriff court and High Court differed because advocates depute did not observe guidance set out in the Crown Office Book of Regulations. Some refused to introduce themselves to young witnesses, to permit a supporter to accompany the child or to agree to the use of CCTV in spite of recommendations by the procurator fiscal and the wishes of the child[175] In relation to CCTV applications, Crown Office guidance noted that the impact of the child's evidence may be reduced when CCTV is used.[176] Although this factor is to be borne in mind in deciding whether to make an application, 'the interests of the child should prevail and such use should not be excluded for this reason alone'.[177] There was a perception that some advocates depute treated such policies on a 'take it or leave it' basis, leading some procurators fiscal to feel that it was preferable for sensitive child witness trials to be dealt with on indictment in the sheriff court.

Recommendation 6: that the Lord Advocate should raise these perceived anomalies with the Home Advocate Depute with a view to their resolution.

---

[173] Handbook on Questioning Children (1994) American Bar Association Center on Children and the Law; A Judicial Primer on Child Sexual Abuse (1994) American Bar Association Center on Children and the Law

[174] For other examples, see the booklet accompanying the NSPCC judicial training video 'A Case for Balance' (1997)

[175] The court must have regard, inter alia, to the views of the child: Criminal Procedure (Scotland) Act 1995, section 271(7) and (8)

[176] K. Murray's research in Scotland found no significant difference between the average conviction rate in CCTV link and non-link cases: Live Television Link (1995) para. 4.43. G. Davies et al. made a similar finding in England and Wales: p. 34, Videotaping Children's Evidence: An Evaluation (1995) Home Office

[177] Book of Regulations 16.122 (1996)

Improving the quality of investigative interviews and the sharing of information to reduce the number of times the child is questioned

The Working Group concluded that significant effort had been invested in joint training of police officers and social workers in investigative interviewing of young witnesses and that overall, standards had improved. However, some procurators fiscal had little confidence in police statements (investigative interviews were not recorded on audio or videotape) and took the view that it was almost always necessary to precognosce young witnesses in solemn procedure cases in order to elicit further information. Police and social work investigative interviews were not conducted within a framework of national guidance: a draft report produced in 1995 by a Working Group set up by the Secretary of State for Scotland and the Lord Advocate has not yet been published in a final version.[178]

Research has highlighted the adverse impact of multiple interviews on the accuracy of the child's account and the level of stress suffered by the child.[179] The greater the number of pre-trial interviewers, the more likely that the process will be rated as harmful.[180] Lord Clyde's Report of the Inquiry into the Removal of Children from Orkney in February 1991 (1992) envisaged a co-ordinated approach that would limit the number of times young witnesses were interviewed. Police and Crown Office policies acknowledge the need to avoid unnecessary interviews because of stress to the child. The research found that those with authority to precognosce were willing to delegate this function (e.g. to precognition officers for the prosecution or to precognition agents for the defence) but not to forgo their right to interview or to adopt other measures to seek the information they needed. Disclosure to the defence of police statements and Crown precognition interviews, which was successful in forestalling some defence precognitions, was exercised selectively and was sometimes said to depend on the procurator fiscal's perception of the defence agent. No overall control was exercised over the total number of interviews, yet prior to trial children could not be reminded of what they said in their initial statement,[181] even after multiple interviews.

The research found that children were not always consulted about whether they wished to be interviewed on their own or accompanied by a supporter. Carers spoke of feeling pressured to consent to the precognoscer seeing the child alone. The Working Group concluded that

---

[178] 'When Children Speak...' Investigating and Interviewing Children in Child Protection

[179] J. Yuille et al. (1993) The Effects of Children Reviewing their Initial Videotaped Interviews on Subsequent Recall for an Interactive Event. Paper for the Ministry of the Attorney General of British Columbia, Canada; J. Henry (1997) System Intervention Trauma to Child Sexual Abuse Victims Following Disclosure, 12 Journal of Interpersonal Violence 499; D. Poole and L. White (1995) Tell Me Again and Again: Stability and change on the repeated testimonies of children and adults. In M. Zaragoza et al (eds.) Memory and Testimony in the Child Witness. Sage Publications

[180] J. Tedesco and S. Schnell (1987) Children's reactions to sex abuse. Investigation and litigation. Child Abuse and Neglect, Vol. 11 pp. 267-72

[181] Permitting witnesses to refresh their memory from their statement before trial is considered good practice in England and Wales: para. 18.3, Statement of National Standards of Witness Care in the Criminal Justice System (1996) Trials Issues Group

guidance was needed concerning the presence of a supporter for the child at prosecution and defence precognitions.[182]

Forthcoming Scottish Office research by David Christie and Susan Moody, based on a small sample of precognition agents, solicitors and witnesses, highlighted the fact that the law presently affords no formal protection to vulnerable witnesses at precognition.[183] There are no rules concerning where precognitions may be taken. The authors noted that in cases where there are multiple accused, it is quite common for witnesses to be precognosced two, three or even more times by different agents. There is no register or directory of precognition agents and few of those contacted by Christie and Moody had received any training. Many were selected without interview and they were not subject to a police check. The authors concluded that it would be possible for a convicted sex offender in the role of precognition agent to gain access to children and took the view that this was an area for urgent concern.

The Scottish Office consultation document 'Towards a Just Conclusion - Vulnerable and Intimidated Witnesses in Scottish Criminal and Civil Cases' noted 'anecdotal examples of defence interviews which caused great distress to children because of the manner in which they were carried out - apparently as a result of ignorance rather than malice'. The consultation document recommended that the Law Society of Scotland be invited, in the interests of minimising trauma for child witnesses and without prejudicing the ability of the defence to prepare its case, to draw up guidance for its members on the interviewing of children.[184]

One aspect of good practice identified by the Working Group's interviews and precognitions pilot was the choice of a person with appropriate skills and training to interview the child. Commenting on this proposal, the Scottish Legal Aid Board's then policy consultant doubted that the Board had a locus to enforce standards set down by the Law Society, but could 'certainly consider allowing charges for acting in accordance with good practice guidance, dependent on what that guidance actually is but unless any rules can actually be incorporated into regulations, I do not think we could try to apply rules ourselves'.[185]

Recommendation 7: that in order to improve the conduct of interviews and precognitions with young witnesses

7.1   The Scottish Office should invite all relevant organisations to co-operate in the development of guidance on the conduct and recording of investigative interviews of children by police officers and social workers, on the basis that implementation of standard guidance would improve the quality and consistency of interviews and assist in reducing the need for others to re-interview the child about the circumstances of the alleged offence

---

[182] The Crown Office Book of Regulations has now been amended to create a presumption that the child witness would be accompanied at precognition by 'a suitable support person' who 'should be warned in advance not to prompt or seek to influence the child in any way' by the procurator fiscal:paras. 16.74 and 16.78 (1998)
[183] The Work of Precognition Agents in Criminal Cases
[184] Para. 4.13 (1998)
[185] Keith Marshall, policy consultant, Scottish Legal Aid Board letter 8.7.1997

7.2 the Crown Office, Association of Chief Police Officers in Scotland and Scottish Children's Reporter Administration should develop consistent policies on the disclosure of police child witness statements and prosecution and reporter precognitions, as greater certainty about disclosure may help to reduce the total number of times that a young witness is interviewed

7.3 the Scottish Children's Reporter Administration should indicate its policy as to when, if at all, reporters should precognosce young witnesses

7.4 the Law Society of Scotland should develop guidance for solicitors on the precognition of young witnesses, for example requiring contact only by prior appointment, conducting the precognition at a location of the child's and carer's choice and ensuring that a supporter chosen by the child is present during the interview. The guidance should address practice where there is more than one accused. A complaints procedure should be established and brought to the attention of witnesses

7.5 the Law Society of Scotland should require solicitors to introduce safeguards to ensure that persons precognoscing young and vulnerable witnesses are screened, have appropriate skills and receive relevant training

7.6 where a solicitor uses an agent with specific skills and training to interview a young witness, the Scottish Legal Aid Board should consider authorising an enhanced fee for this purpose

Identification evidence

Seeing the accused is widely recognised to be the most common source of stress for young witnesses. In the cases studied by the researchers, identification evidence relied on children's involvement in identification parades and dock identification of the accused in court. The research found that some children were required to do both. The police were concerned that recent shifts in procurator fiscal policy would result in an increasing number of children being required to attend parades, even where the accused was a member of the child's immediate household (examples in pilot cases included a brother and a father). In its 1990 report, the Scottish Law Commission observed:

> '... in many instances, identification is not in dispute in the sense that the accused does not seek to challenge that he is the person referred to in a witness's evidence... In such cases, therefore, identification of the accused is no more than a formality... in cases of this sort it should not be necessary for a child to make an in-court identification'.[186]

---
[186] Report on the Evidence of Children and Other Potentially Vulnerable Witnesses, para. 3.12

In light of this finding, the Law Commission made a recommendation for legislative reform which has not as yet been implemented.

An important outcome of the identification pilot was the development of checklists for the officer conducting an identification parade, the officer in charge of the investigation, young witnesses attending parades and their carers. These checklists were well received by officers.

The pilot explored two ways of further reducing the trauma of children attending identification parades: video-recording the parade and showing it to the witness at some later point[187] and allowing the witness to view the parade over a CCTV link. The Working Group acknowledged that further work needed to be done on these options and that the resource implications were considerable.

Recommendation 8: that in order to reduce the stress of young witnesses in relation to identification of the accused:

8.1 the recommendation of the 1990 Scottish Law Commission report on the Evidence of Children and Other Vulnerable Witnesses (paragraph 3.20) should be implemented -

'a) In any case, whether under solemn or summary procedure, where a report of an identification parade or of some other recognised identification procedure has been lodged as a production by the prosecutor, it should be presumed, subject to (b) below, that the person named in the report as having been identified by a witness also named in the report is the person of the same name in the complaint or indictment and answering the charge in court.

(b) The foregoing presumption should arise only where (i) the prosecutor has, not less than 14 days before the trial, served on the accused a copy of the report and a notice of intention to rely on the presumption, and ii) the accused has not given notice of an intention to challenge the facts stated in the report by at least six days before the trial, or by such later time before the trial as the court may in special circumstances allow'

8.2 the Association of Chief Police Officers in Scotland should disseminate the checklists for the officer conducting an identification parade, the officer in charge of the investigation and for young witnesses attending parades and their carers, subject to their further evaluation by the Strathclyde Police

---

[187] Research suggests that identification performance at live and videotaped line-ups is 'virtually identical': B. Cutler et al (1989) Eyewitness Identification from Live Versus Videotaped Line-ups. Forensic Reports, Vol. 2, 93 - 106. Provisions for showing the witness a videotaped parade exist in England and Wales under the Police and Criminal Evidence Act 1984. Over half the English forces have evaluated a computer database of video clips. This system is believed to reduce stress for witnesses, save resources and greatly increase the range of 'stand-ins'. The Times, 3 November 1996

8.3 the Association of Chief Police Officers in Scotland should explore ways to reduce further the trauma of children attending identification parades, including video recording the parade and showing it to the witness at some later point and allowing the witness to view the parade over a CCTV link

The child's familiarisation visit to the court

Professionals, children and their carers were in agreement about the value of the child's familiarisation visit to the court before the trial or children's hearing court proceeding. Many different personnel - principally procurators fiscal and their precognition officers, but also reporters, court staff and court-based social workers - conducted visits and the approach varied very widely. The most helpful visits made the child feel more at ease by ensuring the attendance of the child's supporter, following up on previous explanations about the court process, and allowing children to ask questions and absorb information at their own pace. Children found it particularly helpful when they were able to practise speaking from the witness box or on CCTV. It was an additional benefit if the child could meet the prosecutor taking the trial. The procurator fiscal's child witness unit in particular conducted these visits with sensitivity.

At the other end of the spectrum visits were sometimes rushed or took place just before the child's testimony, and involved little more than standing at the courtroom door with the child and pointing out where the participants would stand or sit. Occasionally, visits were conducted by personnel who were unfamiliar with the concerns of child witnesses or the procedures used in child witness cases and this was perceived as insensitive by children and their carers. Those conducting visits were sometimes unclear about what response could be made to children's most frequently asked question, namely where the accused would be in the courtroom.

Limited advice to procurators fiscal on the conduct of the visit is already provided in the Book of Regulations. This was further developed during the support and preparation pilot in the child witness officer's protocol and also in draft guidance produced by the Scottish Court Service in consultation with other members of the Working Group.

Recommendation 9: that in order to improve the conduct of child witness familiarisation visits to the court:

9.1 the Lord Advocate should invite all those involved in the criminal and civil justice process to agree guidance on the conduct of familiarisation visits

9.2 persons conducting familiarisation visits should receive training based on this guidance which raises awareness of the concerns of young witnesses and their carers and the importance of being able to respond to their questions in a neutral way

9.3 the Lord Advocate should invite judges and sheriffs to ask whether children have had a familiarisation visit and allow some time for this to take place if the child has not already seen a courtroom

The child's rights and pre-trial therapy

Despite policy that the procurator fiscal could not prevent pre-trial therapy, counselling was often discouraged even where it was considered necessary for the child's self-protection. Reporters had no policy guidance on children receiving therapy before giving evidence at court but some discouraged it.[188]

Recommendation 10: that in order to clarify the roles of those making decisions relating to therapy before court proceedings:

10.1 the Crown Office, Scottish Children's Reporter Administration, social work departments, health boards and child welfare organisations should, in consultation with the Law Society of Scotland and Faculty of Advocates, produce a code of practice addressing the provision of therapy before children give evidence

10.2 the code should emphasise that decisions about the timing and the need for therapy can only be taken by those responsible for the welfare of the child and that the interests of children in need of treatment are paramount

10.3 the code should contain advice for therapists about how to avoid undermining children's credibility and reliability or influencing their memory of events or the account they give

Children's hearing court proceedings

The research terms of reference covered both criminal and children's hearing court proceedings. The representation on the Working Group of the Reporter to the Children's Panel (now the Scottish Children's Reporter Administration) added a vital dimension to its deliberations. Unfortunately the pilot studies received no case referrals from reporters concerning children's hearing court proceedings. Reporter interviews highlighted a number of concerns about children's interests that the research was unable to address. These included the increasingly adversarial nature of court proceedings and the need for judicial case management to encourage negotiation between parties so that children's evidence was used only where essential.

Recommendation 11: that The Scottish Office and Scottish Children's Reporter Administration should address the need for research focusing on children's hearing court proceedings.

---

[188] The Crown Prosecution Service and Department of Health produced a code of practice on pre-trial therapy for consultation in February 1999

Publications

In consultation with the Working Group, the CWO wrote a protocol on the support and preparation for court of young witnesses which directed the work she undertook during the pilot project. The protocol was based on research and good practice in Scotland and other jurisdictions. It provided practical guidance on many issues about which social workers and others engaged in child witness preparation had expressed uncertainty during the research, and suggested various ways to identify and address children's concerns about court. NCH Action for Children and Children 1st have offered to publish a version of this document.

In order to provide advice for parents and carers during the pilot initiatives, the Strathclyde Police published the booklet 'Your Child is a Witness' which was developed by the researchers in consultation with the Working Group. This booklet has Crown Office copyright and was published with a local insert containing information on statutory and voluntary agencies in Glasgow. Whereas the Crown Office publications 'Going to court as a witness?' are aimed at children cited as witnesses by the procurator fiscal, the parents' booklet is intended for distribution at an earlier point, soon after offences are reported to the police. It filled a significant gap and was well received. However, supplies are nearly exhausted and efforts need to be made to ensure continuing availability.

The booklet for parents and carers covered only criminal proceedings. Towards the end of the project, The Scottish Office published a series of booklets describing what happens at children's hearings but the comments of parents interviewed for the research suggested there remained a pressing need for guidance for young witnesses and their non-abusing parents or carers in relation to what happens at children's hearings court proceedings.

Recommendation 12: that the Lord Advocate should consider inviting the relevant organisations to discuss publication and distribution of the booklet for parents and carers 'Your Child is a Witness'

Recommendation 13: that NCH Action for Children and Children 1st should continue to consult with the relevant organisations in preparing the guidance on the support and preparation of child witnesses for publication

Recommendation 14: that the Scottish Children's Reporter Administration should develop materials for children and their parents and carers in relation to children's hearing court proceedings

The need for statistics about young witness cases

A key feature of any child witness strategy is the ability to identify cases when they are reported to the police and at all stages as they progress through the justice system. At present, there is no mechanism to do so in either criminal or children's hearing court proceedings.[189] Flagging up is important in order to facilitate planning and to prompt the consideration of appropriate measures. Information is also needed about the volume and type of cases dealt with in order to determine resource requirements. In the future, the Integration of Scottish Criminal Justice Information Systems (ISCJIS) Project will allow all criminal justice agencies to share the same information from the stage when a complaint of a crime is first recorded until final disposal and release from prison.

Crown Office policy gives child witness cases priority but it is unclear whether this applies to every case with a young witness or only to special categories.[190] There are no statistics to indicate how long cases take at each stage.[191] Procurators fiscal have internal targets for case processing and time limits govern the progress of cases at court. Nevertheless, a strategy to reduce delay needs to address the overall time taken by each case from the report to the police to final disposition. Without monitoring, it is impossible to know to what extent delay is a problem; certainly some cases are pending for a long time even before a first court appearance. Monitoring should cover the period from reporting to the police to the submission of the police report and case processing by the procurator fiscal as well as how long the cases take at court. There should also be monitoring of the number of times child witness cases are rescheduled, particularly at the High Court. The procurator fiscal child witness unit advised that 'the High Court usually allocate an early diet but the first trial diet very rarely takes place'.[192] Information is also needed about outcomes: if sex offender registration is to be meaningful, it is vital to know the extent to which cases in which charges are brought result in convictions.[193]

In Scotland, statistics on the duration of proceedings have been produced for the Criminal Justice Forum but are not routinely disseminated. Without national figures for comparison, it will not be possible to determine whether child witness cases in Scotland actually receive priority.

Data collection on forensic medical examinations covers only the numbers of such examinations and where the examinations take place. Additional data is needed to assess compliance with other policy issues, for example whether medical examinations are conducted jointly by forensically trained paediatricians or by a police casualty surgeon together with a

---

[189] Child witness files in the procurator fiscal's office should be 'easily identifiable' (Book of Regulations 16.75; 16.77) but were often undesignated. The procurator fiscal's computer had a field to identify 'witnesses under 16' which was not used. In a scheme outside Glasgow, the procurator fiscal and sheriff clerk used coloured stickers to highlight child witness cases

[190] The Crown Prosecution Service Inspectorate has recommended that the CPS and police agree a common definition of child witness cases to which provisions for priority status apply. Para. 5.8, Report on Cases Involving Child Witnesses (1998) Thematic Report 1/98

[191] The Criminal Justice Consultative Council of England and Wales has instituted a national monitoring exercise for child witness cases in which data is collected about prosecution case processing before the case first appears in court as well as court disposition times

[192] Memorandum on the priority of cases 3.8.98

[193] Statistics on charges and their outcomes in relation to offences against children should be published 'to enable policy makers... to see the extent and nature of the problem, to identify any trends and assess the need for action'. Para. 20.30 People Like Us: the Report of the Review of Safeguards for Children Living Away from Home (1997) Department of Health and Welsh Office

paediatrician. Only a small proportion of examinations result in clinically significant findings and concerns were raised during the research that medical examinations by police casualty surgeons were sometimes overused.[194] During the course of the study, the majority of forensic medical examinations of children were not conducted in appropriately equipped hospital premises, by specially trained physicians in accordance with best practice laid down in inter-agency policies. There were problems in complying with children's requests to be examined by a female doctor. By the end of the study, provisions were being put in place for examinations of children under five to be conducted according to best practice guidance.

Recommendation 15: that in order to inform decision-making about the level of need and resource allocation, relevant agencies should jointly establish mechanisms for the collection and publication of statistics on:

15.1 the number of young witnesses in the criminal and children's hearing court proceedings system

15.2 how long each organisation takes to process young witness cases at each stage of proceedings

15.3 how often cases are rescheduled for diets and the reasons why this happens

15.4 the incidence of forensic medical examinations and compliance with inter-agency policy on the manner in which they should be conducted

Recommendation 16: that in order to facilitate the prioritisation of cases, relevant agencies should:

16.1 agree a common definition of which young witness cases should receive priority

16.2 identify mechanisms for flagging up young witness cases to ensure that they receive appropriate treatment and to avoid delay at all stages

16.3 adopt a 'culture of urgency' in which the priority status of young witness cases is highlighted on files and correspondence

---

[194] Police or prosecution requests for a forensic medical examination should be subject to medical review: in a project in Lothian, only 42 per cent of referrals for assessment to a hospital-based service proceeded to a medical examination: J. Mok et al (1998) The Joint Paediatric - Forensic Examination in Child Abuse. Child Abuse Review Vol. 7:194-203

MEMBERS OF THE WORKING GROUP 1995-1998 (THOSE WHO WERE MEMBERS AT THE LAST MEETING OF THE GROUP ARE SHOWN IN BOLD)

Len Higson (Chaired the Working Group) Crown Office (now Regional Procurator Fiscal)

Elish Angiolini, Procurator Fiscal Service
Ouaine Bain, Strathclyde Social Work Department
Fiona Bevan, Scottish Courts Administration
Betty Bott, Procurator Fiscal Service and, latterly, Crown Office
William Campbell, Chief Superintendent, Strathclyde Police
Alison Di Rollo, Procurator Fiscal Service
Anne Duffy, Victim Support Scotland
John Fotheringham, solicitor, Law Society of Scotland
Greg Gallagher, Glasgow City Council Social Work Department
Ian Gilmour, Strathclyde/Glasgow City Social Work Departments
Dennis Gough, Glasgow City Council Social Work Department
Moyra Hawthorn, NCH Action for Children
Dr Jean Herbison, consultant paediatrician, Yorkhill Hospital
Philip Jackson, Strathclyde Reporter to the Children's Panel
Alan Johnston, Scottish Courts Administration
James Johnstone, Detective Chief Superintendent, Strathclyde Police
William Johnston, Detective Chief Inspector, Strathclyde Police
Bruce Kennedy, Detective Inspector, Strathclyde Police
Paul Langan, solicitor, Law Society of Scotland
Donald MacDonald, Chief Superintendent, Strathclyde Police
Pam McFarlane, Scottish Court Service
Gerry McLaughlin, Glasgow City Council Social Work Department
Dr David McLay, chief medical officer, Strathclyde Police
Kenneth Morrison, Chief Superintendent, Strathclyde Police
David Nicoll, Sheriff Clerk's Department, Glasgow Sheriff Court
Susan Raeburn QC, Sheriff, Sheriffdom of Glasgow and Strathkelvin, Sheriffs' Association
Jackie Robeson, Scottish Children's Reporters Administration
Dr Anne Sutton, consultant paediatrician
David Turnbull, NCH Action for Children
Geri Watt, Crown Office and Procurator Fiscal Service
John Watt, Procurator Fiscal Service
Gordon Williams, Procurator Fiscal Service.

Research Advisors

Dr Joe Curran, Scottish Office Central Research Unit
Susan McVie, Scottish Office Central Research Unit
Fiona Fraser, Scottish Office Central Research Unit

Joyce Plotnikoff, Research Consultant
Richard Woolfson, Research Consultant
Una Plotnikoff, Research Consultant

Child Witness Officer

Ouaine Bain, NCH Action for Children and Children 1st

The Working Group had secretarial assistance from Gary Aitken, Clare Bone, Lesley Dick, Melanie Golding, Geoff Main and **Claire Wilkinson.**

CRU RESEARCH - PUBLICATIONS LIST FROM 1999

Poor Housing and Ill Health: A Summary of Research Evidence: Housing Research Branch. (1999) (£2.50)

One Stop Shop Arrangements for Development Related Local Authority Functions: Centre for Planning Research, School of Town and Regional Planning, University of Dundee. (1999) (£5.00)
Summary available: Development Department Research Findings No.63

Research on Walking: System Three. (1999) (£5.00)

Resolving Neighbour Disputes Through Mediation in Scotland: Centre for Criminological and Legal research, University of Sheffield. (1999) (£4.00)
Summary available: Development Department Research Findings No.64

Literature Review of Social Exclusion: Centre for Urban and Regional Studies, University of Birmingham. (1999) (£5.00)

Mentally Disordered Offenders and Criminal Proceedings: Dr M Burman, Department of Sociology and Ms C Connelly, School of Law, University of Glasgow. (1999) (£7.50)

Evaluation of Experimental Bail Supervision Schemes: Ewen McCaig and Jeremy Hardin, MVA Consultancy. (1999) (£6.00)
Summary available: Social Work Research Findings No.28

An Evaluation of the 1997/98 Keep Warm This Winter Campaign: Simon Anderson and Becki Sawyer, System 3. (1999) (£5.00)
Summary available: Social Work Research Findings No.29

Attitudes Towards Crime, Victimisation and the Police in Scotland: A Comparison of White and Ethnic Minority Views: Jason Ditton, Jon Bannister, Stephen Farrall & Elizabeth Gilchrist`, Scottish Centre for Criminology. (1999) (£5.00)
Summary available: Crime and Criminal Justice Research Findings No.28

The Safer Cities Programme in Scotland – Evaluation of the Aberdeen (North East) Safer Cities Project: MVA. (1999) (£5.00)

Review of National Planning Policy Guidelines: Land Use Consultants. (1999) (£5.00)
Summary available: Development Department Research Findings No.65

Development Department Research Programme 1999-2000. (1999) (Free)

Environment Group Research Programme 1999-2000. (1999) (Free)

Rural Policy Research Programme 1999-2000. (1999) (Free)

Referrals between Advice Agencies and Solicitors: Carole Millar Research. (1999) (£5.00)
Summary available: Legal Studies Research Findings No.21

Life Sentence Prisoners in Scotland: Diane Machin, Nicola Coghill, Liz Levy. (1999) (£3.50)
Summary available: Crime and Criminal Justice Research Findings No.29

Report on a Conference on Domestic Violence in Scotland, Scottish Police College, Tulliallan: The Scottish Office, The Health Education Board for Scotland, The Convention of Scottish Local Authorities, The Scottish Needs Assessment Programme. (1999) (£5.00)

Making it Safe to Speak? Witness Intimidation and Protection in Strathclyde: Nicholas Fyfe, Heather McKay, University of Strathclyde. (1999) (£7.50)f

Supporting Court Users: The Pilot In-Court Advice Project in Edinburgh Sheriff Court: Elaine Samuel, Department of Social Policy, University of Edinburgh. (1999) (£5.00)
Summary available: Legal Studies Research Findings No. 22

The Role of Mediation in Family Disputes in Scotland: Jane Lewis, Social and Community Planning Research. (1999) (£5.00)
Summary available: Legal Studies Research Findings No. 23

Research on Women's Issues in Scotland: An Overview: Esther Breitenbach. (1999) (Free)
Summary only available: Women's Issues Research Findings No. 1

Women in Decision-Making in Scotland: A Review of Research: Fiona Myers, University of Edinburgh. (1999) (Free)
Summary only available: Women's Issues Research Findings No. 2

Evaluation of the Debtors (Scotland) Act 1987: Study of Individual Creditors: Debbie Headrick and Alison Platts. (1999) (£5.00)
Summary available: Legal Studies Research Findings No. 10

Evaluation of the Debtors (Scotland) Act 1987: Study of Commercial Creditors: Alison Platts. (1999) (£5.00)
Summary available: Legal Studies Research Findings No. 11

Evaluation of the Debtors (Scotland) Act 1987: Study of Debtors: David Whyte. (1999) (£5.00)
Summary available: Legal Studies Research Findings No. 12

Evaluation of the Debtors (Scotland) Act 1987: Study of Facilitators: Andrew Fleming. (1999) (£5.00)
Summary available: Legal Studies Research Findings No. 13

Evaluation of the Debtors (Scotland) Act 1987: Survey of Poindings and Warrant Sales: Andrew Fleming. (1999) (£5.00)
Summary available: Legal Studies Research Findings No. 14)

Evaluation of the Debtors (Scotland) Act 1987: Survey of Payment Actions in the Sheriff Court: Andrew Fleming, Alison Platts. (1999) (£5.00)
Summary available: Legal Studies Research Findings No. 15

Evaluation of the Debtors (Scotland) Act 1987: Analysis of Diligence Statistics: Andrew Fleming, Alison Platts. (1999) (£5.00)
Summary available: Legal Studies Research Findings No. 16

Evaluation of the Debtors (Scotland) Act 1987: Overview: Alison Platts. (1999) (£5.00)

Looking After Children in Scotland: Susanne Wheelaghan, Malcolm Hill, Moira Borland, Lydia Lambert and John Triseliotis. (1999) (£5.00)
Summary available: Social Work Research Findings No.30

The Evaluation of Children's Hearings in Scotland: Children in Focus: Lorraine Waterhouse, Janice McGhee, Nancy Loucks, Bill Whyte & Helen Kay
Summary available: Social Work Research Findings No.31

Taking Account of Victims in the Criminal Justice System: A Review of the Literature: Andrew Sanders. (1999) (£5.00)
Summary available: Social Work Research Findings No.32

Social Inclusion Bulletin No.1: (1999) (Free)

Geese and their Interactions with Agriculture and the Environment: JS Kirby, M Owen & JM Rowcliffe. (1999) (£10.00)
Summary available: Countryside and Natural Heritage Research Findings No.1

The Recording of Wildlife Crime in Scotland: Ed Conway. (1999) (£10.00)
Summary available: Countryside and Natural Heritage Research Findings No.2

Socio-Economic Benefits from Natura 2000: GF Broom, JR Crabtree, D Roberts & G Hill. (1999) (£5.00)
Summary available: Countryside and Natural Heritage Research Findings No.3

Crime and the Farming Community: The Scottish Farm Crime Survey 1998: Andra Laird, Sue Granville & Ruth Montgomery. (1999) (£10.00)
Summary available: Agricultural Policy Co-ordination and Rural Development Research Findings No.1

New Ideas in Rural Development No 7: Community Development Agents in Rural Scotland: Lynn Watkins & Alison Brown. (1999) (£2.50)
Summary available: Agricultural Policy Co-ordination and Rural Development Research Findings No.2

New Ideas in Rural Development No 8: Tackling Crime in Rural Scotland: Mary-Ann Smyth. (1999) (£2.50)
Summary available: Agricultural Policy Co-ordination and Rural Development Research Findings No.3

Study of the Impact of Migration in Rural Scotland: Professor Allan Findlay, Dr David Short, Dr Aileen Stockdale, Anne Findlay, Lin N Li, Lorna Philip. (1999) (£10.00)
Summary available: Agricultural Policy Co-ordination and Rural Development Research Findings No.4

An Electoral System for Scottish Local Government: Modelling Some Alternatives: John Curtice. (1999) (£5.00)

Writing for the CRU Research Series: Ann Millar, Sue Morris & Alison Platts. (1999) (Free)

The Effect of Closed Circuit Television on Recorded Crime Rates and Public Concern about Crime in Glasgow: Jason Ditton, Emma Short, Samuel Phillips, Clive Norris & Gary Armstrong. (1999) (£5.00)
Summary available: Crime and Criminal Justice Research Findings No.30

Working with Persistent Juvenile Offenders: An Evaluation of the Apex Cueten Project: David Lobley & David Smith. (1999) (£5.00)
Summary available: Crime and Criminal Justice Research Findings No.31

The Role and Effectiveness of Community Councils with Regard to Community Consultation: Robina Goodlad, John Flint, Ade Kearns, Margaret Keoghan, Ronan Paddison & Mike Raco. (1999) (£5.00)

Perceptions of Local Government: A Report of Focus Group Research: Carole Millar Research. (1999) (£5.00)

Supporting Parenting in Scotland: Sheila Henderson. (1999) (£5.00)
Summary available: Social Work Research Findings No.33

Investigation of Knife Stab Characteristics: I. Biomechanics of Knife Stab Attacks; II. Development of Body Tissue Simulant: Bioengineering Unit & Department of Mechanical Engineering, University of Strathclyde. (1999) (£5.00)

City-Wide Urban Regeneration: Lessons from Good Practice: Professor Michael Carley & Karryn Kirk, School of Planning & Housing, Heriot-Watt University. (1999) (£5.00)
Summary available: Development Department Research Findings No.66

An Examination of Unsuccessful Priority Partnership Area Bids: Peter Taylor, Ivan Turok & Annette Hastings, Department of Urban Studies, University of Glasgow. (1999) (£5.00)
Summary available: Development Department Research Findings No.67

The Community Impact of Traffic Calming Schemes: Ross Silcock Ltd, Social Research Associates. (1999) (£10.00)
Summary available: Development Department Research Findings No.68

The People's Panel in Scotland: Wave 1 (June-September 1998): Dr Nuala Gormley. (1999) (Free)
Summary only available: General Research Findings No.1

The People's Panel in Scotland: Wave 2 (August-November 1998): Dr Nfuala Gormley. (1999) (Free)
Summary only available: General Research Findings No.2

Evaluation of Prevention of Environmental Pollution from Agricultural Activity (PEPFAA) Code: Peter Evans, Market Research Scotland. (1999) (£5.00)
Summary available: General Research Findings No.3

Review of Safer Routes to School in Scotland: Derek Halden Consultancy in association with David McGuigan. (1999) (£5.00)

Climate Change: Scottish Implications Scoping Study: Andrew Kerr & Simon Allen, University of Edinburgh; Simon Shackley, UMIST; Ronnie Milne, Institute of Terrestrial Ecology. (1999) (£5.00)
Summary available: Environment Group Research Findings No.5

City-Wide Urban Regeneration: Lessons from Good Practice: Professor Michael Carley & Karryn Kirk. (1999) (£5.00
Summary available: Development Department Research Findings No.66

An Examination of Unsuccessful Priority Partnership Area Bids: Peter Taylor, Ivan Turok & Annette Hastings. (1999) (£5.00)
Summary available: Development Department Research Findings No.67

The Children's Traffic Club in Scotland: Katie Bryan-Brown & Gordon Harland. (1999) (£5.00)
Summary available: Development Department Research Findings No.69

An Evaluation of the New Life for Urban Scotland Initiative in Castlemilk, Ferguslie Park, Wester Hailes and Whitfield: Cambridge Policy Consultants. (1999) (£10.00)
Summary available: Development Department Research Findings No.70

National Monitoring and Interim Evaluation of the Rough Sleepers Initiative in Scotland: Anne Yanetta & Hilary Third (School of Planning & Housing, ECA/Heriot-Watt University) & Isobel Anderson (HPPU, University of Stirling). (1999) (£5.00)
Summary available: Development Department Research Findings No.71

Social Inclusion Research Bulletin No.2. (1999) (Free)

Costs in the Planning Service: Paula Gilder Consulting. (1999) (£5.00
Summary available: Development Department Research Findings No.72

Evaluation of the Teenwise Alcohol Projects: Simon Anderson & Beckie Sawyer. (1999) (£6.00)
Summary available: Crime and Criminal Justice Research Findings No.34

The Work of Precognition Agents in Criminal Cases: David J Christie & Susan R Moody (University of Dundee). (1999) (£5.00)
Summary available: Crime and Criminal Justice Research Findings No.32

Counting the Cost: Crime Against Business in Scotland: John Burrows, Simon Anderson, Joshua Bamfield, Matt Hopkins & Dave Ingram. (1999) (£10.00)
Summaries available: Crime and Criminal Justice Research Findings No's. 35, 38, 39 & 40.

Park and Ride in Scotland: Transport Research Laboratory and Strathclyde Passenger Transport. (1999) (£5.00)
Summary available: Development Department Research Findings No.74

Understanding Offending Among Young People: Janet Jamieson, Gill McIvor & Cathy Murray. (1999) (£16.00)
Summary available: Social Work Research Findings No.37

The View from Arthur's Seat: A Literature Review of Housing and Support Options 'Beyond Scotland': Ken Simons & Debbie Watson (Norah Fry Research Centre, University of Bristol). (1999) (£5.00)

"If You Don't Ask You Don't Get": Review of Services to People with Learning Disabilities: The Views of People who use Services and their Carers: Kirsten Stalker, Liz Cadogan, Margaret Petrie, Chris Jones, Jill Murray (Scottish Human Services). (1999) (£5.00)

Diversion from Prosecution to Social Work and Other Service Agencies: Evaluation of the 100% Funding Pilot Programmes: Monica Barry & Gill McIvor (University of Stirling). (1999) (£5.00)
Summary available: Crime and Criminal Justice Research Findings No.37

Council Tax Collection Arrangements in Scotland, England & Wales: Institute of Revenues, Rating and Valuation. (1999) (£5.00)
Summary available: Development Department Research Findings No.80 (2000)

Why People don't Drive Cars: Sue Granville & Andra Laird (George Street Research). (1999) (£5.00)F

Support at Home – Views of Older People about their Needs and Access to Services: Charlotte MacDonald (University of Stirling). (1999) (£14.00)
Summary available: Social Work Research Findings No.35

Transport Provision for Disabled People in Scotland: Sheila Henderson and Brian Henderson, Reid Howie Associates. (1999) (£10.00)
Summary available: Development Department Research Findings No. 76

Community Mediation in Scotland – A Study of Implementation: Robert E Mackay and Amanda J Brown, University of Dundee. (1999) (£5.00)
Summary available: Legal Studies Research Findings No.24

Drug Misuse in Scotland: Simon Anderson & Martin Frischer. (2000) (£5.00)
Summary available: Crime and Criminal Justice Research Findings No.17

Support for Majority and Minority Ethnic Groups at Home – Older People's Perspectives: Alison Bowes and Charlotte MacDonald
Summary only available: Social Work Research Findings No.36

Intermediate Diets, First Diets and Agreement of Evidence in Criminal Cases: An Evaluation: Frazer McCallum & Professor Peter Duff (Aberdeen University Faculty of Law). (2000) (£5.00)
Summary available: Crime and Criminal Justice Research Findings No.42

The Experience of Violence and Harassment of Gay Men in the City of Edinburgh: Colin Morrison & Andrew Mackay (The TASC Agency). (2000) (£5.00)
Summary available: Crime and Criminal Justice Research Findings No.41

The Development of the Scottish Partnership on Domestic Abuse and Recent Work in Scotland: Dr Sheila Henderson (Reid Howie Associates). (2000) (£5.00)

Children, Young People and Crime in Britain and Ireland: From Exclusion to Inclusion - 1998 Conference Papers: Monica Barry (University of Stirling), Joe Connolly (Action for Children), Olwyn Burke, Dr J Curran (Central Research Unit, Scottish Executive). (2000) (£5.00)

Overview of Written Evidence Received as Part of the Review of the Public Health Function in Scotland :
Summary available only: General Research Findings No.4

Assessment of the Voter Education Campaign for the Scottish Parliament Elections: (Scotland Office Publication): Andra Laird, Sue Granville & Jo Fawcett (George Street Research). (2000) (£5.00)

Review of the Experience of Community Councils as Statutory Consultees on Planning Applications: Ewan McCraig, MVA. (2000) (£5.00)
Summary available Development Department Research Findings No.77

Family Support and Community Care: A Study of South Asian Older People: Alison Bowes and Naira Dar with the assistance of Archana Srivastava (University of Stirling). (2000) (£6.00)
Summary available: Social Work Research Findings No.38

Review of the Experience of Community Councils as Statutory Consultees on Planning Applications: Ewan McCraig, MVA. (2000) (£5.00)
Summary Available Development Department Research Finding No.77

Development Department Research 2000-2001: (2000) (Free)

An Evaluation of the SACRO (Fife) Young Offender Mediation Project: Becki Sawyer, System 3. (2000) (£5.00)
Summary available: Crime and Criminal Justice Research Findings No.43

Environment Group Research Programme 2000-2001: (2000) (Free)

Social Inclusion Bulletin No.3: (2000) (Free)

Road Safety in the Scottish Curriculum: Tony Graham, ODS Ltd. (2000) (£5.00)
Summary available: Development Department Research Findings No.78

The Role of Information and Communications Technology in Road Safety Education: BITER – The British Institute of Traffic Education Research. (2000) (£5.00)
Summary available: Development Department Research Findings No.79

Evaluation of Scottish Road Safety Campaign Travel Packs: Sharon Reid, Andra Laird & Jo Fawcett. (2000) (£5.00)
Summary available: Development Department Research Findings No.82

Audit of ICT Initiatives: In Social Inclusion Partnerships and Working for Communities Pathfinders in Scotland: Joanna Gilliatt, Doug Maclean & Jenny Brogden, Lambda Research & Consultancy Ltd. (2000) (£5.00)

Researching Ethnic Minorities in Scotland: Reid-Howie Associates. (2000) (Free)

A Comparative Evaluation of Greenways and Conventional Bus Lanes: Colin Buchanan and Partners. (2000) (£5.00)
Summary available: Development Department Research Findings No.83

Advertising Planning Proposals: James Barr Planning Consultants. (2000) (£5.00)
Summary available: Development Department Research Findings No.84

Developing Markets for Recyclable Materials in Scotland: Prioritising Materials: Enviros RIS Ltd in association with Clean Washington Centre. (2000) (Free).
Summary only available: Environment Group Research Findings No.6

The Development of the Scottish Partnership on Domestic Abuse and recent Work in Scotland: Dr S Henderson, Reid Howie Associates. (2000) (£5.00).

Evaluation of the Airborne Initiative (Scotland): Gill McIvor, Vernon Gayle, Kirstina Moodie, Stirling University and Ann Netten, University of Kent. (2000) (£5.00)
Summary available: Crime and Criminal Justice Research Finding No.45

A Review of the Research Literature on Serious and Sexual Offenders: Clare Connelly and Shanti Williamson, University of Glasgow. (2000) (£8.00).
Summary available: Crime and Criminal Justice Research Finding No.46

The Quality of Services in Rural Scotland: Steven Hope, Simon Anderson and Becki Sawyer, System Three.

Summary available: Rural Affairs Research Finding No.5.

Social Exclusion in Rural Areas; A Literature Review and Conceptual Framework: Mark Shuckshank and Lorna Philip, University of Aberdeen. (2000) (£10).
Summary available: Rural Affairs Research Finding No.6.

Charities Report: **1. Scottish Charity Legislation; Full Report** (2000) (£15.00).
2. Scottish Charity Legislation; Executive Summary (2000) (Free).
3. Scottish Charity Legislation; Annexes (2000) (£5.00).
4. Public Charitable Collections (2000) ((£5.00).
5. Public Trusts and Educational Endowments (2000) (£5.00).
University of Dundee.
Summary available: Legal Studies Research Finding 26

Meeting in the Middle: A Study of Solicitors' and Mediators Divorce Practice: Fiona Myers and Fran Wasoff. University of Edinburgh. (2000) (£5.00)
Summary available: Legal Studies Research Finding No.25.F

Real Burdens: Survey of Owner Occupiers' Understanding of Title Conditions: Andra Laird and Emma Peden, George Street Research (2000) (£5.00)
Summary available: Legal Studies Research Finding No.27

Survey of Complainers to the Scottish Legal Services Ombudsman: The Customer Management Consultancy Ltd (2000) (£5.00)

An Evaluation of Electronically Monitored Restriction of Liberty Orders: david Lobley and David Smith, Lancaster University (2000) (£5.00)
Summary available: Crime and Criminal Justice Research Finding No.47

Interviewing and Drug Testing of Arrestees in Scotland: A Pilot Study of the Arrestee Drug Abuse Monitoring (ADAM) Methodology: Neil McKeganey, Clare Connelly, Lesley Reid & John Norrie University of Glasgow, Janusz Knepil Gartnavel General Hospital Glasgow. (2000) (£5.00)
Summary available: Crime and Criminal Justice Research Finding No 48

The Role of Sport in Regenerating Deprived Areas: Fred Coalter with Mary Allison and John Taylor, Centre for Lesisure Research (2000) (£5.00)
Summary available: Development Department Research Finding No 86

The Role of Pre-Application Discussions and Guidance in Planning: Peter Gibson and Robert Stevenson, The Customer Management Consultancy Ltd (2000) (£5.00)
Summary available: Development Department Research Finding No 85

Huts "and Hutters" in Scotland: Research Consultancy Services (2000) (£5.00)

Research Finding Only: Motivations to Public Service: Development Department RF No. 87. Sue Granville and Andra Laird, George Street Research (2000) (£0.00)

Research Finding Only: The What, Where and When of Being a Councillor: Development Department RF No. 88. Paolo Vestri and Stephen Fitzpatrick, Scottish Local Government Information Unit. (2000) (£0.00)

Future Patterns of Retailing in Scotland: John Dawson (Professor of Marketing, The University of Edinburgh and Visiting Professor ESADE, Barcelona). (2000) (£5.00)
Summary available: Development Department Research Findings No.91

Women's Issues in Local Partnership Working: Gill Scott, Gill Long, Usha Brown, Jane McKenzie, Scottish Poverty Information Unit). (2000) (£5.00)
Summary available: Social Inclusion Research Findings No.1f

Moving On: A Survey of Travellers' Views: Delia Lomax, Sharon Lancaster (School of Planning & Housing, ECA/Heriot-Watt University) and Patrick Gray (Housing Research Centre, Magee Collecte, University of Ulster). (2000) (£5.00)
Summary available: Development Department Research Findings No.94

Monitoring the Children (Scotland) Act 1995: Pilot Study: Jeremy Hardin, MVA; Professor Alastair Bissett-Johnson, University of Dundee; Shona Main, University of Dundee. (2000) (£5.00)

Accessibility: Review of Measuring Techniques and their application: Derek Halden; David McGuigan; Andrew Nisbet and Alan McKinnon (Derek Halden Consultancy). (2000) (£5.00)
Summary Available: Development Department Research Findings No.89

Research into the Basis for Local and National Estimates of the Number of BTS Houses in Scotland: DTZ Pieda Consulting in association with Dr J I Ansell. (2000) (£5.00)

Summary Available: Development Department Research Findings No.90

Pedestrian Perceptions of Road Crossing Facilities: J M Sharples and J P Fletcher. (2000) (£5.00)
Summary Available: Development Department Research Findings No.92

Social Inclusion Research Bulletin No.4: (2000) (Free)

Research on Repeat Victimisation in Scotland: Mandy Shaw & Ken Pease, Applied Criminology Group, University of Huddersfield (2000) (£5.00)
Summary available: Crime & Criminal Justice Research Findings No.44

Social Work and Criminal Justice: the Longer Term Impact of Supervision: Gill McIvor and Monica Barry, Social Work Research Centre, University of Stirling (2000) (£5.00)
Summary available: Crime and Criminal Justice Research Findings No 50

An Evaluation of the Parent Information Programme: Gillian Mayes, John Gilles, Greame Wilson, University of Glasgow, Raymond Macdonald, Glasgow Caledonian University (2000) (£5.00)
Summary available: Legal Studies Research Findings No 29

The Use of Civil Legal Remedies for Neighbour Nuisance in Scotland: Rowland Atkinson, Tom Mullen, and Suzie Scott, University of Glasgow (2000) (£8.00)
Summary Available: Legal Studies RF No 28

Research Finding Only: Results of the Scottish Executive Staff Survey 2000: General Research RF No 5, Patrick Barron and Andrew Fleming, (2000) (£0.00)

Research Findings Only: The 2000 Scottish Crime Survey: First Results: Crime and Criminal Justice RF No 51, MVA Ltd, (2000) (£0.00)

Research Finding Only: Postal Witness Citation and Countermanding: An Evaluation of the Mechanised System Piloted in Glasgow, Ayr and Lanark: Crime and Criminal Justice RF No 49, Ian Clark, (2000), (£0.00)

Solicitor Advocates in Scotland: A Statistical Analysis: Debbie Headrick, (2000) (£5.00)
Summary Available: Legal Studies RF No 32

Evaluation of the Local Rural Partnership Scheme: Louise Brown Research, (2001) (£5.00)
Summary Available: Rural Studies RF No. 7

Solicitor Advocates in Scotland: The Impact on Clients: Gerard Hanlon and John Jackson, (2000) (£5.00)
Summary Available: Legal Studies RF No 33

Research Findings Only: Solicitor Advocates in Scotland: The Impact on the Legal Profession: Legal Studies RF No 34, Karen Kerner (2000) (£0.00)

Solicitor Advocates in Scotland: A Research Overview: Alison Platts, (2000) (£5.00)
Summary Available, Legal Studies RF No 35

Credit Union Development Activity in Scotland: Centre for Economic Development and Area Regeneration (CEDAR) and The Planning Exchange, (2000), (£5.00)

The People's Panels in Scotland's Social Inclusion Partnerships: Guidance for SIPs: Jo Fawcett, Sue Granville and Andra Laird, George Street Research, (2000), (free)

Local Authority Waste Management Costs Study: Enviros Aspinwall, (2000), (£5.00)
Summary Available, Environment Group RF No.7

Assessment of Innovative Approaches to Testing Community Opinion: Andra Laird, Jo Fawcett, Fiona Rait and Sharon Reid, George Street Research Ltd, (2000), (£5.00)
Summary Available, Social Inclusion RF, No.2

Green Commuter Plans: Do They Work?: Tom Rye and David McGuigan, Napier University, Transport Research Unit, (2000), (£.5.00)
Summary Available, Development Department RF No. 95

Using People's Juries in Social Inclusion Partnerships: Guidance for SIPs: Robin Clarke, Ruth Rennie, Clare Delap, and Vicki Coombe, (2000), (free).
Summary Available, Development Department RF No. 97: Peoples's Juries in Social Inclusion Partnerships: A Pilot Project.

Women and Transport: Moving Forward: Reid-Howie Associates, (2000), (£5.00)
Summary Available, Development Department RF No. 98

Public Assistance to Rural Land in Scotland: Richard Cowell, Gillian Bristow, Terry Marsden, and Alex Franclin, (Cardiff University), (2001) (£5.00)
Summary Available: Rural Studies No 8

Further information on any of the above is available by contacting:

Dr A Scott
Chief Research Officer
The Scottish Office Central Research Unit
Room J1-5
Saughton House
Broomhouse Drive
Edinburgh
EH11 3XA

or by accessing the World Wide Website: www.scotland.gov.uk